Adult Entertainment

by Elaine May

A SAMUEL FRENCH ACTING EDITION

SAMUEL FRENCH

FOUNDED 1830

SAMUELFRENCH.COM

ISBN   978-0-573-62988-4   Printed   in   U.S.A.   #3835

IMPORTANT BILLING AND CREDIT REQUIREMENTS

All producers of ADULT ENTERTAINMENT *must* give credit to the Author of the Play in all programs distributed in connection with performances of the Play and in all instances in which the title of the Play appears for purposes of advertising, publicizing or otherwise exploiting the Play and/or a production. The name of the Author *must* appear on a separate line on which no other name appears, immediately following the title, and *must* appear in size of type not less than fifty percent the size of the title type.

In addition, the following credit *must* appear in all programs distributed in connection with the Work:

ADULT ENTERTAINMENT was first presented in New York City on December 11, 2002 at Variety Arts Theatre

Produced by
JULIAN SCHLOSSBERG   ROY FURMAN   BEN SPRECHER
JIM FANTACI   BILL ROLLNICK & NANCY ELLISON   TED LACHOWICZ
In association with AARON LEVY

Opening night: December 11, 2002

VARIETY ARTS THEATRE

Under the direction of BEN SPRECHER and WILLIAM P. MILLER

JULIAN SCHLOSSBERG   ROY FURMAN   BEN SPRECHER

JIM FANTACI   BILL ROLLNICK & NANCY ELLISON   TED LACHOWICZ

in association with **AARON LEVY**

present

DANNY AIELLO   JEANNIE BERLIN

in

ADULT ENTERTAINMENT

by

ELAINE MAY

with

MARY BIRDSONG   BRANDON DEMERY   ERIC ELICE   LINDA HALASKA

JEN COOPER DAVIS   ALFRED KARL   REESE MADIGAN

Scenic Design	Costume Design	Lighting Design	Sound Design
NEIL PATEL	SUZY BENZINGER	PHIL MONAT	T. RICHARD FITZGERALD
Video Design	Wig Design	Dance Assistant	Original Music by
CARL CASELLA	PAUL HUNTLEY	JODI MOCCIA	BRYAN LOUISELLE

Casting By	Technical Supervision	Production Stage Manager
HOWARD/SCHECTER/MELTZER	KEN KENEALLY & ROB CONOVER	JANE GREY

Associate Producer	Press Representative	General Manager
JILL FURMAN	THE PUBLICITY OFFICE	PETER BOGYO

Directed by

STANLEY DONEN

Originally presented at Rich Forum, Stamford Center for the Arts, November, 2002.

The producers wish to express their appreciation to Theatre Development Fund for its support of this production

ACT I

(Both sides of the stage are concealed by glider panels. In the center is a two-tiered bench on which three porn stars and a man in a suit are doing a public access TV show. Behind them is a monitor on which the show is being televised. Below the stage, where the orchestra would be, is the cameraman, who is actually shooting the show. The three semi-clad porn stars and the man in the suit are wearing identical black armbands.)

HEIDI-THE-HO. Hi. This is yours truly Heidi-The-Ho and tonight we're going to pay tribute to legendary film maker Marty Akens who passed away last Friday. With me tonight to talk about Marty are Miz Frosty Moons, Mr. Jumbo J. and Marty's brother Mr. Guy Akens. Let's start with you, Jumbo. How long did you and Marty work together?

JIMBO. Jimbo. About a year. We made seventy-five movies together. He was a fantastic director.

HEIDI-THE-HO. Fantastic. And you changed your name?

JIMBO. No, it was always Jimbo. "Jumbo" was the name of my last movie.

HEIDI-THE-HO. I saw that. You were great.

JIMBO. My name was Jumbo for one movie but then I found out there already was another Jumbo and my agent said that it could cause a lot of confusion so I changed my name back to my real name which is Jimbo.

HEIDI-THE-HO. Oh. So Jimbo was always your real name and now it still is.

JIMBO. Yes.

HEIDI-THE-HO. What was the last movie you made with Marty, Jimbo?

JIMBO. "Jumbo."

HEIDI-THE-HO. That was so great.

JIMBO. Yeah.

HEIDI-THE-HO. Frosty Moons, you worked with Marty the longest.

FROSTY MOONS. Yes.

HEIDI-THE-HO. How long was that?

FROSTY MOONS. Oh ... let's see ... he took me on as a fluffer when I was fifteen which was a great break because now there's no budget for fluffers so guys just use their girlfriends. But I had the opportunity to learn my craft with Marty and the late, great Ricky Dicky Tavy until—I think until Marty finished shooting *Willy's Wonga* ...

JIMBO. Oh, my God. That was the first movie I auditioned for.

FROSTY MOONS. Oh, you're kidding! So that's about a year ... and then I auditioned and got a six week gig on *Days to Come* ...

HEIDI-THE-HO. *(Into camera.)* For you ho-watchers who sleep all day, that's a legitimate soap that's still on now....

FROSTY MOONS. ... and someone saw me in that and I got a part in a series: "Three Is a Crowd" ...

HEIDI-THE-HO. *(To camera; pointing at FROSTY MOONS.)* Melissa Ryan in *Three Is a Crowd*, thank you everybody. Thank you, Mr. Cameraman. This is Melissa, ho-watchers!

(The others clap.)

FROSTY MOONS. ... and then after five years *Crowd* got canceled ... so that's six years....

HEIDI-THE-HO. But not six years that you worked with Marty.

FROSTY MOONS. No, at that point I had still just worked with Marty for one year but when I got canceled I was nowhere and I went back to him and he said—and I never forgot this—"Welcome back,

Frosty, you've learned your craft" and he put me in front of the camera this time and I worked with him until Ricky died and I quit Adult so ... what was your question?

HEIDI-THE-HO. I forgot.

JIMBO. "How long did you work with Marty?"

FROSTY MOONS. Oh. Altogether I guess ... pretty long.

HEIDI-THE-HO. That's such a great story. Jimbo, you starred in Marty's legendary movie *Between Her Legs*.

FROSTY MOONS. Oh, I loved that movie. That scene where everybody finds out where the car keys are ...

JIMBO. Oh, don't give it away.

HEIDI-THE-HO. You were fantastic in that.

JIMBO. Thank you. *Between Her Legs* was really a breakthrough movie for me because up to then I was only cast as ... *(Making "quote" marks.)* ... "the stud" because I have ten inches. Or twelve inches depending where you measure from—but it was like that was all I could do.

FROSTY MOONS. Yeah, you get type cast.

JIMBO. I'm not complaining. My johnson gave me my start. But I made nearly 120 movies and the only lines I ever got to say were like "Take it all" or "Tell your sister to turn around" ... just made up lines. Like I couldn't tell her sister to turn around by myself. But *Between Her Legs* gave me a chance to play a character. I had a limp. I mean, I didn't have a lot of lines but I had interesting scenes. And my performance earned me two AVN nominations this year, best group and best anal.

HEIDI-THE-HO. So you could be a big winner.

JIMBO. Yeah, but win or lose it's an honor just to be nominated.

FROSTY MOONS. *Between Her Legs* is my favorite because it's about something—like *The Devil in Miss Jones* or *Deep Throat*. I mean, it has something to say. The car keys were like a metaphor. Like the apple in Eden.

HEIDI-THE-HO. *(After a tiny pause.)* Yes.

FROSTY MOONS. It's more than a piece of fruit but it's a piece of fruit, too, so that makes it interesting.

HEIDI-THE-HO. Yes.

FROSTY MOONS. I think Marty was trying to get back to the golden days when pornos played in real theaters....

JIMBO. That must have been so incredible—when there was still glamour.

HEIDI-THE-HO. Yes. Where are you appearing now, Jimbo?

JIMBO. Mr. Peepers, exit 18 off the Jersey Turnpike on Fridays and Saturdays, and I'll be dancing there until the 30th.

HEIDI-THE-HO. *(To camera.)* So get out to the Jersey Turnpike this weekend, all you ho-watchers, and see a great show. *(To the man in the suit.)* Guy, you were Marty's brother.

GUY. Yes. I still am.

HEIDI-THE-HO. And you're a director, too, right?

GUY. Yes. But I direct more in legitimate regional theater. I'm probably a little more into acting and story than Marty was. Marty was more filmic.

HEIDI-THE-HO. He was great.

GUY. I'm also a producer and a writer but I don't take a writing credit. I punched up a lot of Marty's movies, and I'm the one who co-wrote *Between Her Legs*. There were no car keys to look for in the movie originally. I put that in.

THE OTHERS. "No kidding!" "Shut the front door!"

HEIDI-THE-HO. What was it like working with Marty behind the scenes? Was it like ... working? Or ... what?

GUY. Marty was very work oriented. Completely. He was like an alcoholic. But with work.

FROSTY MOONS. Yes. He was just about the project.

HEIDI-THE-HO. *(Laughs inappropriately.)* That's great.

JIMBO. *(To GUY.)* So what was that like? When they told you he was dead. That must have been so ... like ... "what's happening to my head?"

GUY. Yeah. It was a surprise. But the good part is we weren't close.

HEIDI-THE-HO. Okay, we're live and waiting for your phone calls. Call us here at 212-782-U-f-me. Tell us what you think about the great Marty Akens ... or anything. Just give us a call. Cuddle up to the phone and say "Hi, Ho" ... Yes. Hello ... you're on the air.

VOICE #1. Hi, Ho.

HEIDI-THE-HO. Hi.

VOICE #1. This is Chuck from New Jersey and I have a question for Jimbo.

JIMBO. Hi, Chuck.

VOICE #1. I saw you in *Jumbo* with Vixen Fox. You were spectacular.

JIMBO. Thanks.

VOICE #1. Was that a real beer bottle?

JIMBO. Yeah.

VOICE #1. Okay.

HEIDI-THE-HO. Thanks for calling.... Hi.... Mr. Caller, you're on the air.

VOICE #3. Hi, Ho.

HEIDI-THE-HO. Hi. You're on the air.

VOICE #3. This is for Frosty.

FROSTY MOONS. Thanks.

VOICE #3. You were great as Melissa, Frosty.

FROSTY MOONS. Thanks.

VOICE #3. I never watched it again after you were gone.

FROSTY MOONS. Well, it was canceled.

VOICE #3. I really miss that show.

FROSTY MOONS. Me too.

HEIDI-THE-HO. Okay. Thanks for calling.... Hi, you're on the air.

VOICE. Hi, baby.

HEIDI-THE-HO. Vixen! Hi.

VIXEN'S VOICE. Hi, everyone!

THE OTHERS. Hi! Hi, Vixen!

HEIDI-THE-HO. *(To camera.)* Hey, ho-watchers. It's the fabulous Vixen Fox.

VIXEN'S VOICE. Just Vixen. I don't use "Fox" anymore.

HEIDI-THE-HO. Where are you dancing now, Miz Vixen?

VIXEN'S VOICE. I'm at Guns and Barrels for the rest of the month. And then at The Dangling Participle during August.

JIMBO. I played The Dangling Participle. It's fabulous.

VIXEN'S VOICE. Hi, Jimbo.

JIMBO. Hi, honey.

FROSTY MOONS. Vixen, it's Frosty.

VIXEN'S VOICE. I know. I'm watching the show.

FROSTY MOONS. We're all here for Marty.

VIXEN'S VOICE. I know. I'm watching the show. *Three Is a Crowd* is on Nick at Nite, did you know that?

FROSTY MOONS. Yeah. Someone said that.

VIXEN'S VOICE. It comes on around three right after *My Favorite Martian.*

FROSTY MOONS. Yeah. You know, that guy died who played the Martian.

VIXEN'S VOICE. Yeah. You should take advantage of that, Frosty.

FROSTY MOONS. Of that he died?

VIXEN'S VOICE. No. Of the show. You're like a star. You're a legit name. Like Traci Lords but in reverse.

FROSTY MOONS. In reverse of Traci Lords?

HEIDI-THE-HO. Okay. Great to talk to you, Vixen. Okay, that's it for our show. Remember for private, nasty calls with the Ho ho-self dial 1-900-TALKOFF and I will answer! And I hear our music coming—so let's dance.

(The three guests wave as the glider panel closes and a prerecorded HEIDI-THE-HO is projected on it. The words 1-900-TALKOFF $4.95-A-MINUTE—MUST BE 18 flash on as she sings.)

HEIDI-THE-HO. *(Prerecorded.)*
Walkin'—the walk with you, baby,
Talkin'—the talk with you, baby,
Walkin' and talkin'
And eatin' box lunch with you.

Walkin' ho-hum,
Talkin' so dumb,
Eatin' yum-yum,
Walkin' and talkin' and talkin' and walkin'
And eatin' box lunch with you.

Gotta walk to get to the picnic,
Gotta talk to pass the time,
But lunch is what I really want
So I'm just waiting till I'm ...

Walkin'—the walk with you, baby,
Talkin'—the talk with you, baby,
Walkin' and talkin' and talkin' and walkin'
And talkin' and walkin' and walkin' and talkin'
And eatin'—box lunch with you.

(The song ends. The R glider panel opens to reveal VIXEN in her white living room, talking to GUY, HEIDI-THE-HO, JIMBO and FROSTY MOONS, who are now in street clothes.)

VIXEN. The thing is everyone wants to see someone legit getting off. You could do a movie as Melissa Ryan and call it *Melissa Goes South* ... or *Saving Ryan's Privates* ... or something that gets one of Melissa's names in the title.

FROSTY MOONS. I was way younger when I played Melissa.

VIXEN. Well, that could be part of the movie. Melissa gets older, time passes that we didn't see because the series was canceled. And then we see her again and she's Frosty. That's what's so great. Frosty is Melissa.

GUY. But is that legal? To just steal a character from a television series.

VIXEN. It's not the character you're stealing. It's just the name. Anyone can change their name. I could change my name to Melissa Ryan.

FROSTY MOONS. And then could I sue you?

VIXEN. No. That's my point. You can't. Because it would be my name. And we could all be in the movie with you. Because we're all on top now. Jimbo's just coming off *Jumbo*, I'm just coming off *Hannah Bell Licked Her*, Heidi's like an icon on late night public access—

HEIDI-THE-HO. That's true. I was actually called an icon.

GUY. And what would I do?

VIXEN. You'd be like Marty was ... like a writer-director-producer. And you could also fill in when there's like two guys in a scene, or if Jimbo can't get it up or gets sick....

JIMBO. Hey, sick or well, I'm wood. You know that.

VIXEN. Oh, yeah, but if we needed more than two guys—like for a group scene—you and Guy could put on different make-up and wigs and play all the characters.

JIMBO. Oh, I would love that. And one of my characters could wear an eye patch.

HEIDI-THE-HO. That would be fabulous.

VIXEN. The important thing is that it's just us and we only have to split the profits five ways. And we don't work for anyone else.

JIMBO. What do you mean? Who'll pay us?

VIXEN. No one. We'll be paid out of profits—like a company.

HEIDI-THE-HO. Oh. But who'll put up the money for the movie?

GUY. Well, if no one gets paid the movie costs almost zero to shoot. I have Marty's equipment and I can hold the camera ... and if I have to be in a scene I can just set the focus and run in front of the lens.

VIXEN. That's so great of Marty to leave you his equipment.

GUY. Well, he didn't officially leave it to me but he was shooting in a garage in Newark and I have the keys. *(Beginning to see it.)* And, you know, distribution might be a "no sweat" deal. Melissa Ryan and Vixen and Heidi-the-Ho and Jimbo all in the same movie? There could be a real "want to see."

JIMBO. But what if there isn't any profits? I mean, I make pretty good money doing movies for Attaboy and Bonanza.

VIXEN. So do I. I can make up to a thousand a day and last year—which was one of my best—I made 200,000 including photo sales, but so what? Half of that goes for taxes and ten per cent goes to my agent off the top so that's 90,000 left and I have to keep getting tested and I pay my own health insurance and I have to keep up my body and my hair and this apartment and my fucking teeth cost a fortune and I send my mother twelve thousand a year so I end up keeping like—20,000 for living and coke and booze and clothes and rent and when I hit sagtime I won't have anything saved. Hey, I'm younger than all of you but I still know that later is gonna last longer than now.

FROSTY MOONS. Yeah. It lasts way longer than now. I was younger than anyone when I started and now I'm older than anyone. And I'm gonna be older longer than I was younger because older just keeps on happening until you die ... and that's a long time with nothing to sell, Jimbo.

JIMBO. Oh, man ... I don't know.

GUY. Hey, you're a talented guy, Jimbo, don't you want to show it?

HEIDI-THE-HO. And think of what we'll save by only working with each other and not having to get tested every two weeks.

JIMBO. What do you mean? We have to get tested. What if we pork someone new off the set?

HEIDI-THE-HO. Well, we can't.

JIMBO. We can't? That's impossible. We won't have any life.

VIXEN. Aren't you still with Ari?

JIMBO. Yeah.

VIXEN. Well?

JUMBO. Well, even if I'm still with Ari that doesn't mean he's just with me.

HEIDI-THE-HO. Wear a condom. Make Ari wear a condom. I make guys wear condoms for hand jobs.

JIMBO. Ari hates that. We both hate that.

VIXEN. Don't you want to be someone, Jimbo? Don't you want to have the chance to be a real actor? Isn't it worth wearing a condom to finally get a shot at a career?

(There is a long pause.)

JIMBO. *(Slowly.)* Yeah. It is.

VIXEN. Well, then come on.

FROSTY MOONS. You could do character things....

HEIDI-THE-HO. You could wear glasses ...

VIXEN. Right.

JIMBO. ... and maybe ... maybe I could have a scar.

HEIDI-THE-HO. Yeah. That could be touching if you have a scar. Like maybe you were in prison.

FROSTY MOONS. And our company could have a name.

HEIDI-THE-HO.	JIMBO.	GUY.
Oh, right!	A name!	Something hot!

ALL. Hot ... \ Hot Times \ Hot ... things \ Hot ... \ Hot ... \ Burning! \ Burning hot! \ Fire-hot! \ Firecrackers! Fireworks!

VIXEN. Fireworks! But with an X! w-o-r-x.

HEIDI-THE-HO. That's good! I like that.

GUY. How about with three x's. W-o-r-x-xx.

VIXEN. That's better.

ALL. Great! That's great, Guy. Fire-triplex-worxxx!

GUY. I'll write an outline.

VIXEN. No, I don't think you should do that. Because then it will be like all the other movies we make. I think you should write the whole thing out. Like a regular movie.

GUY. The whole thing?

VIXEN. Yeah, because it's about Melissa. So it has to pick up stuff from the series .....

FROSTY MOONS. ... and it has to say what happened to the other characters.

HEIDI-THE-HO. They could be dead, her parents could be dead, and maybe she's got a kid and her husband is gone a lot and he's a scumbag so she's taking on guys....

FROSTY MOONS. Oh, that's so sad.

JIMBO. I like that. I like that we get to be sad, too.

VIXEN. And maybe ....

GUY. Alright. Enough already. I got enough suggestions. This is gonna be one hell of a tough script to write. I've got maybe two solid weeks of work ahead of me ... but I'm excited. I'm challenged. I'm ready to tango!

(The glider panel closes behind him and he whips out a tiny laptop, typing rhythmically as he sings:)

GUY.
Tay-ay-ayngo!
Oh, I am ready to
Tay-ay-ayngo,
Ba-da-bum-ba-da-beem
ba-da-bingo-bango,
Is tango ready for me?
I'm challenged,
I'm challenged and excited,
My fire's all ignited,
My bonnet has a bee!

(He steps behind the glider panel—)

GUY'S VOICE.
Is tango ready for me?
We'll see, we'll see, we'll see!

(He steps out again holding a script—)

GUY.
If Tango's ready forrrr-------ME!

*(The panel opens to reveal a garage filled with cartons, movie equip-
ment, car parts, posters, etc. The cast sits holding scripts as GUY
reads.)*

GUY. "It is the living room of Melissa, lovely, in her 30's, wearing expensive lingerie. Her maid Tina enters."

HEIDI-THE-HO. *(Reading.)* "Your lover, Mr. Carlysle is here.
And he's brought another man."

FROSTY MOONS. *(Reading.)* "My God, Ted is still warm in his
grave and already Carlysle is demanding a manage a ... " ... There's
a typo.

GUY. That's "trois." Menage a trois. It means three on a match in
French.

FROSTY MOONS. It's spelled "troys."

GUY. But it's pronounced trois. I'd like to hear my whole script
read without interruptions. I'm shooting this reading.

FROSTY MOONS. "My God, Ted is still warm in his grave and
already Carlysle is demanding a menage a trois. I'm glad my mother
is dead so she didn't have to see this."

HEIDI-THE-HO. "So should I say you're in?"

FROSTY MOONS. "Yes. I can't say no to Carlysle or he'll re-
fuse to pay for little Benny's boarding school. Help me change into
something more comfortable, will you, Tina?"

HEIDI-THE-HO. "Okay."

GUY. *(Reading.)* "Tina starts helping Melissa out of her satin teddy. As she sees Melissa's breasts she suddenly cups them."

FROSTY MOONS. "Tina! What are you doing."

HEIDI-THE-HO. "Sorry."

GUY. *(Reading.)* "Tina lets go of her breasts and takes the rest of Melissa's teddy off and then begins feeling her up all over."

FROSTY MOONS. "Tina! No, no, no. Tina stop."

HEIDI-THE-HO. "I can't stop now."

GUY. "Tina goes down on Melissa. Just as Melissa is coming Carlysle" —that's me— "enters with another man who is wearing a neck brace. Carlysle: Hey, what's going on here? I'm sorry about this, Tom."

JIMBO. "That's all right. Mind if I join the party?"

GUY. "Well, okay. And I guess I will, too. But be careful of your neck."

FROSTY MOONS. "No, no. What are you doing?"

GUY. "Tom begins doing Tina. Melissa goes down on Carlysle...." *(He looks up.)* I'll work out the blocking later. *(Back to the script.)* "The door opens and the principal of Benny's boarding school comes in. She is wearing a tailored suit and glasses."

VIXEN. "The door was open so I just came in. I'm the principal of Benny's boarding school. Hey, what's going on here?"

GUY. *(Reading.)* "At first she is outraged, but then she gets horny watching and begins playing with herself and finally takes off her clothes and joins the party. Scene two. Close-up—Tom's wad. Camera pulls back to reveal ...."

HEIDI-THE-HO. I don't have any part.

GUY. What?

HEIDI-THE-HO. I hardly have any three lines.

GUY. You want more lines? Okay. Write this in. After Carlysle says "What's going on here?" you say "I'm Tina, Mr. Carlysle. We didn't meet before because I was on vacation."

HEIDI-THE-HO. That's dumb.

GUY. What?

HEIDI-THE-HO. I'm gonna stop eating her to introduce myself?

That's dumb.

JIMBO. I don't have any lines. I have one line.

GUY. And a neck brace.

JIMBO. Yeah, but the neck brace doesn't go anywhere. I just wear it.

FROSTY MOONS. And I keep talking about Benny but then his principal walks in on us and I don't even talk to her.

GUY. Because by that time you're so worked up.

VIXEN. And I'm a school principal but after I say "What's going on here?" I just stand there playing with myself. I'm not even pissed that no one says hello.

GUY. Hey, this is a porno. What are you all talking about?

JIMBO. But if it can't show us acting what's the point of not doing regular pornos.

GUY. You get a few more lines. And a lot more money.

JIMBO. I make good money now. I'm doing this for a career. I'm not fighting all day with Ari about wearing a bag to make a few more bucks saying dumb lines.

GUY. Hey, you think you can write it better? You write it.

VIXEN. And what will you do? We can get anyone to put up equipment and direct us. You have to write for your piece.

GUY. Well, I don't know how to write what you're talking about. I don't know what you would say that's different.

HEIDI-THE-HO. I'd say "Oh, Miss Melissa, I remember when you were just a girl and you were going to the prom with Bud...."

FROSTY MOONS. I remember that episode. I'm afraid Bud will laugh when he sees me all dressed up because up to then I've been a tomboy....

GUY. Good. Hey! Maybe we dissolve to a flashback of prom night: Let's improv this. Bud and the family see Melissa all dressed up for the first time and they're surprised—okay, everybody be someone. Jimbo—be Bud.

JIMBO. Hey! Melissa! You're all dressed up.

FROSTY MOONS. Yeah. How do I look ... sis?

VIXEN. You look ... really ... all dressed up. Doesn't she, Tina?

HEIDI-THE-HO. Yeah. And just yesterday she was a tomboy.

GUY. Yeah. Well, Melissa ... don't get home too late, little lady.

FROSTY MOONS. I won't, Dad.

GUY. Perfect. And then—fuzzy focus, we jump back to the present and pick up with Heidi saying "Your lover Mr. Carlysle is here. And he's brought another man."

VIXEN. That's no good, Guy. We can't just make up things for the flashback.

HEIDI-THE-HO. You gotta write us acting things. We gotta have lines.

FROSTY MOONS. On the series they gave us whole speeches.

GUY. Hey—that's the best I can do. If you think it's such shit bring someone in to punch it up. I'll give him a piece of my piece. But it has to be a real writer.

HEIDI-THE-HO. I know a real writer, not a published writer or anything, but he's written stuff and he studied writing at a workshop....

GUY. And he's gonna write for you for nothing?

VIXEN. I thought he was gonna get a piece of your piece.

GUY. Well, he's not. Hey, fuck it. You tell me I have to write it, then I write it, then it's "Oh, is this your writing? We hate it. Give up a piece of your piece so we can get a real writer...."

VIXEN. You offered to give up a ....

FROSTY MOONS. You said you wanted ....

GUY. Yeah, yeah, but you know what this is all about and so do I. You don't think I have any talent. Well, I'll tell you something, and this goes especially for you, Vixen, when a movie gets started you better have somebody without talent keeping his eye on the ball. And that's where I come in. You know why the shittiest movie director makes more than any writer? Because without someone saying "be here at nine—we'll work until two" no one would show up. A director is the glue that keeps it together. And you know why the shittiest producer makes more than the shittiest director? Because he's the guy who says to the director "We can't afford to come in at nine because then we'll have to buy breakfast and lunch. Tell 'em to be here at eleven." And when you got someone like me—someone who says "be here at eleven and bring your lunch" all in one package—you got more than glue. You got cement.

(There is a pause.)

VIXEN. Okay, if Heidi's got a writer, I think we should all chip in for him.

JIMBO. Wait a minute ....

VIXEN. Just a piece of our piece.

JIMBO. But then we won't have as big a piece.

FROSTY MOONS. But we'll have a writer.

GUY. Wait a minute. What if we don't like his work? Who is this writer?

HEIDI-THE-HO. He's my cameraman.

(They stare at her.)

VIXEN. Your cameraman!

FROSTY MOONS. The guy who shoots your show?

GUY. "Mr. Cameraman"?

HEIDI-THE-HO. Yeah. He's a fantastic writer. And he went to Yale.

VIXEN. Yale college?

HEIDI-THE-HO. Yeah.

FROSTY MOONS. You're kidding. The Yale college that's like Harvard? That college?

HEIDI-THE-HO. Yeah. He just got out a few years ago.

GUY. And he's shooting your show for public access?

HEIDI-THE-HO. Yeah. Because he's writing and he needs loose hours. And he's fussy, man. He thinks everything is shit but my show. He says shooting my show reinforces his sense of irony. Isn't that a great word? "Reinforces"?

FROSTY MOONS. But why would he write this? It's just a little movie.

HEIDI-THE-HO. That's the only kind he says he'll write. And when I show him the tape we made and we show him Marty's garage with all the equipment—

GUY. And he'll understand that it's an adult movie....

HEIDI-THE-HO. Well, duh. He's not gonna think it's an after-school special. It's starring us.

(Blackout. A single light comes up on GERRY.)

GERRY. Let me start by saying that Heidi has explained your concept and I've read Guy's script and looked at the tape of the first reading. I think this is a movie about expectations. And, how, ulti-mately, these expectations are crushed and become transformed into the hard-eyed cynicism that is the mask for disappointment. *(As he speaks additional lights come up revealing the rest of the cast sitting in the garage, listening.)* The theme is hope, the dynamic is trust, the villain—and the hero—is reality.

(There is a frozen pause.)

FROSTY MOONS. Is it still about Melissa?

GERRY. Oh, yes. I'm not changing the characters or the idea.

HEIDI-THE-HO. Gerry liked our improv.

GERRY. Very much. Because it demonstrates the national myth of the 50's: that no adolescent who says gosh has had sex and all chil-dren are ten until they're sixteen.

VIXEN. Frosty's series was in the 70's.

GERRY. It doesn't matter. I'm talking in terms of metaphor and cultural and national myth. All Americans define themselves in terms of the 50's. Everything we consider a deviation from the norm is actu-ally a deviation from the values of the 50's. That is the norm we yearn for and denounce, make fun of and embrace, rebel against and insist on in our unconscious. The irony is that these values only came into existence in 1945 and were only followed until 1965. No other country had them, no other country was young enough to believe in it's own innocence and scrappiness except, possibly, Australia. Yes, Jimbo?

JIMBO. Do I ... when I enter in the first scene ... do I still wear a neck brace?

GERRY. Good question. No. You don't wear a neck brace, Jimbo. Because you now enter as Bud, the son of the boy who used to date Melissa.

JIMBO. Then ... who plays the Bud who used to date Melissa?

GERRY. You do. You play both the young Bud who used to date Melissa and Bud's son.

JIMBO. But ... then ... who play's the old Bud ... Bud's dad?

GERRY. *(Carefully.)* You do.

JIMBO. Oh, man. I'm getting scared.

GERRY. Look, everything starts just the same. Tina the maid tells Melissa she remembers when she was young bla-bla-bla. And we flash back to when Melissa was sixteen and Bud came to take her to the prom bla-bla-bla. Then we go back to the present and the maid tells Melissa—the older Melissa now .... *(JIMBO's hand shoots up.)* Yes. You don't have to raise your hand, Jimbo.

JIMBO. Can whoever I play wear a neck brace?

GERRY. *(After a moment.)* Yes. *(To FROSTY MOONS.)* Turn to the scene after the flashback when Bud Jr. enters ... page eleven in your scripts, sixth speech down, beginning with "Oh, my God...." *(There is a rustle of paper. A pause.)* Okay? Frosty?

FROSTY MOONS. Fine, Gerry.

GERRY. No, I mean "okay" say your line.

FROSTY MOONS. Oh. "Oh, my God ...."

JIMBO. "What is it?"

FROSTY MOONS. "You look so much like ... like someone I knew when I was young."

JIMBO. "Who?"

(He frowns at the shortness of his line.)

FROSTY MOONS. "It doesn't matter. That was in another country, And besides, the wench is dead." *(She looks up.)* Is that ...?

GERRY. It's a quotation from *The Jew of Malta*. Just say it for now. Then I'll give you the play to read.

FROSTY MOONS. "But that was in another country; And besides, the wench is dead."

JIMBO. *(Shaking his head sadly.)* "Ah, Marlowe."

GERRY. No, no. *(JIMBO stares at him.)* She's not Marlowe. Marlowe is the man who wrote *The Jew of Malta*. You hear her say "But that was in another country" bla-bla-bla, and you recognize the quote as something written by Marlowe, who's been dead for hundreds of years, and you say: "Ah! Marlowe" as in "Ah-hah! I recognize that quote. It's from a play by Marlowe."

JIMBO. But ... how is anyone going to know I mean all that if all I say is "Ah, Marlowe"?

GERRY. *(After a moment; grimly.)* I'll rewrite the line. Let's go on. Frosty?

FROSTY MOONS. Yes, Gerry?

GERRY. Let's go on. Let's take it from Jimbo's line ... whatever it turns out to be.

FROSTY MOONS. From "Yes. You know his work?"

GERRY. Yes.

FROSTY MOONS. "Yes. You know his work?"

JIMBO. "Very well. My father used to read it with the girl he loved when he was a boy. He left me the book when he died. Laughs bitterly. I thought he was going to leave me money."

GERRY. *(Quietly.)* Don't read what's in the parenthesis, Jimbo.

JIMBO. What?

GERRY. Don't read what's inside the parenthesis.

FROSTY MOONS. ... The two C's that face each other.

JIMBO. So don't read "laughs bitterly"?

GERRY. No. Just do it. *(Studying him.)* You've done seventy-two movies. Haven't you ever seen a script before?

JIMBO. Yeah. But not one with parenthesis.

GERRY. Melissa, from "You know Marlowe?"

FROSTY MOONS. "You know Marlowe?"

JIMBO. "Yes. My father used to read him with the girl he loved when he was a boy. He left me his books when he died. Laughs bit—" *(Breaks off; laughs bitterly.)* "I thought he was going to leave me money."

GERRY. Guy, will you pick it up with ...

GUY. I know where. I was taking a pause. "Well, let's start what we'll come for, Melissa." *(He looks up.)* Shouldn't it be let's start what we came for, Melissa?

GERRY. No. It's a play on the word "come," and I'm also toying with tenses. "Let's start what we will eventually come for" i.e. fucking, is what Carlysle means. But I'm using the present tense to describe Carlysle's expectation in the future so that the audience will be momentarily confused.

GUY. Good idea. That's a big plus when you're whacking off to a porno.

GERRY. Guy ... I understand that you may be resentful about the changes I've made in your script ....

GUY. I'm not resentful, Gerry. But as the director and co-writer I have the right to question your changes. I worked with plays for many years, you know, in regional and dinner theaters.

(GERRY looks at them for several moments, then lowers his script.)

GERRY. Alright, let me explain what I'm trying to do here. I want this to be a hardcore porn movie that's completely different from any porn movie ever done, a kind of *Merchant and Ivory* porn movie—but better because it's not an adaptation. *(To GUY.)* I want you to direct a movie that's ambiguous and fresh so your directing will get critical attention. *(To the CAST.)* I want you to act in a movie that has literary pretensions and complexity—a movie in which porn is a kind of metaphor. Do you know what I mean by metaphor?

FROSTY MOONS. Yes. It's more than porn but it's porn, too, so that makes it interesting.

GERRY. *(He thinks; then:)* Yes.

JIMBO. But isn't porn pretty interesting? I mean people buy a lot of porn. So they must be interested in it.

GERRY. Yes, but Heidi said you were trying to do more than porn. You were trying to show you can act. Well, what I learned at Yale was—if you want to be noticed you have to do something unique, something true, something that involves your heart and your mind and your soul—not just your body. And I want to help you do that. But you have to use your minds. I want you to ask questions. But I want you to think, too. And I want you to think like artists. Jimbo, you want to be a real actor? Buy a real script and read it. Heidi, you're going to be a maid? Study maids, talk to them, see what their life is like. Frosty, you were Melissa. You can look into your own mind, your own feelings, and see what Melissa would feel like now. Vixen, you're going to play Kitten, Melissa's little sister. Jimbo you're Bud. Look at *Father Knows Best*, read *Our Town*. Investigate what dating was like for two inexperienced adolescents in a loving, fictional family.

VIXEN. You know, I actually didn't have much experience dating when I was a kid. I was so busy doing movies.

GERRY. Excellent. And another thing I want you to try—whatever you're on: weed, crack, powder, ecstasy, meth, pills, poppers, booze, whatever—cut down. If you're going to give a great performance you have to stay in touch with your feelings, and not just the good feelings that come from dope, you have to stay in touch with your pain, too. You have to stay in touch with the truth.

(Everyone's hand shoots up.)

JIMBO. But … you're not saying stop altogether....
GERRY. No. Just cut down. *(The hands drop.)* It'll be tough, but being an artist is tough. Let's make the tough choices.

(The glider panel closes. A prerecorded FROSTY MOONS is projected on it.)

FROSTY MOONS. *(Prerecorded.)*
Sometimes you need a good mechanic,
To make your engine throb,
And you look like a good mechanic,
I like to watch you do your job,
It so cool, baby, cool,
The way you ...
Use your tool,
The way you ...
Sink your shaft,
Right up to the haft,
The way you turn your screw,
The way you do your do,
I like the way the oil is burning,
I like the ping the pistons make,
Pressure's high and wheels are churning,
Step on the gas—forget the brake,
Cause it's hot, baby, hot,
Oh, my God, it's hot,
Oh, wow,
It's hotter now,
Yes, it's hot and how!
Boiling, burning, baking, churning,
Roasting, toasting, sizzling hot!
And that's cool.

(The song ends; the panel opens to reveal FROSTY MOONS et al on

the Ho Show.)

HEIDI-THE-HO. That was great. We're back and we're live with
Miz Frosty "Melissa" Moons, Mr. Jumbo Jimbo, Miz Vixen, and
famed director Guy Akens. Frosty, you were talking before the break
about *The Jew of Malta.*
FROSTY MOONS. Yes.
HEIDI-THE-HO. So what's that all about.
FROSTY MOONS. It's this play that I have some lines from in
my new movie and the writer asked me to read it so I could better understand my part so I did. *(To GERRY who is offstage.)* And it was so
hard I had to buy this other book that explains it. The whole play is
written in ...
 GERRY'S VOICE OFF. Stop talking to me.
FROSTY MOONS. Oh. Okay. *(To the others.)* ... the whole play
is written in little broken lines like song lyrics ... and it has a lot of
"thou"s and "thee"s in it like the Bible.
VIXEN. Because it was written so long ago.
FROSTY MOONS. Yeah, it's really old. I don't even know
where Malta is. I thought it was in the Philippines but no one in the
play says for sure.
JIMBO. Are there Jews in the Philippines?
VIXEN. Oh, sure. There are Jews everywhere. There are Jews in
Mexico.
GUY. *(Nervously.)* Well, let's not talk about Jews anymore.
Frosty, tell us some more about the movie.
FROSTY MOONS. Well, we're all in it. And you're the director ....
HEIDI-THE-HO. Mr. Guy Akens, ho-watchers; the great Marty
Akens' live brother.
JIMBO. I'm surprised that there were plays about Jews way back
then.
VIXEN. Why? There are Jews in the Bible.
JIMBO. Oh, that's right. What am I thinking. The Jews killed Jesus.
GUY. Hey! That's never been proved. What are we talking about

here?

FROSTY MOONS. Well, it doesn't matter. It was so long ago. Anyway, this play is about ... I think it's about this Jew who gets these two guys who want to shag his daughter to kill each other because one of their fathers took his money and he's got this thing about money and he says things like it doesn't matter if you kill someone so long as he isn't Jewish and he has his own daughter killed because she wants to stop being Jewish and become a nun.

HEIDI-THE-HO. That's great. Okay, we're live and waiting for your phone calls. Call us here at 212-782-U-f-me. Tell us what you think about Frosty and Jimbo and Vixen and the great Guy Akens ... or anything. Just give us a call. Cuddle up to the phone and say "Hi, Ho." ... Yes. Hello.... You're on the air....

VOICE #1. Hi, Ho.

HEIDI-THE-HO. Hi.

VOICE #1. This is for Vixen.

JIMBO. Thanks.

VOICE #1. You're beautiful, Vixen.

VIXEN. Thanks.

VOICE #1. You dropped the Fox.

VIXEN. Yeah.

VOICE #1. How come.

VIXEN. I don't know.

VOICE #1. Okay. You're beautiful.

VIXEN. Thanks.

HEIDI-THE-HO. Okay. Thanks for calling.... Hi. You're on the air.... Hello?

VOICE #2. Hi, Ho.

HEIDI-THE-HO. Hi. You're on the air.

VOICE #2. This is for Frosty Moons.

FROSTY MOONS. Thanks.

VOICE #2. I think, when you say it doesn't matter that the Jews killed Jesus that it does matter.

FROSTY MOONS. Oh, right. I just meant it was like thousands

and thousands of years ago ... so, you know, like ... it's over.

VOICE #2. Yeah, but it's still terrible.

FROSTY MOONS. Well, yeah. Sure.

VOICE #2. But you said it didn't matter.

FROSTY MOONS. Well, I just meant that it was so long ago that it didn't matter to the story I was telling now.

VOICE #2. But it still matters.

FROSTY MOONS. Oh, yeah.

VOICE #2. It matters to Jesus.

FROSTY MOONS. Right.

VOICE #2. It would matter to Melissa.

FROSTY MOONS. Oh, sure.

HEIDI-THE-HO. Okay. Thanks for calling.

VOICE #2. Okay, thanks. You're going to hell, Frosty.

(She hangs up. There is a dial tone. They sit for a moment, stunned ... then the end music starts.)

HEIDI-THE-HO. Okay, and that's our music, ho-watchers ... remember for private calls with the Ho ho-self dial 1-900-TALKOFF and I will answer!—okay, wave goodbye everyone.

(They wave ... as the music fades and the monitor goes dark. FROSTY MOONS puts her head in her hands.

VIXEN. It's one moron. Forget it.

JIMBO. It's just one moron, right, Gerry?

GERRY. Right. Although now that we're going to start promoting the movie we should probably know what not to mention. And high on that list is Jesus.

GUY. And Jews. I mean, my heart was in my mouth when you started on Jews....

FROSTY MOONS. What do you mean? I didn't say anything about Jews. I was just describing the play. This is a famous play that's thousands of years old. If it said something bad about Jews, Jews wouldn't let it be published.

GUY. "Jews wouldn't let it get published?" Are you crazy? Where the hell have you been? That's the kind of thing I expect Jimbo to say.

JIMBO. What is?

VIXEN. Oh, this is all so stupid. First of all, Jews don't watch Heidi....

GUY. How do you know what Jews watch. I know plenty of Jews who watch Heidi.

HEIDI-THE-HO. No kidding.

FROSTY MOONS. But I didn't say anything bad. Oh, man, I really feel terrible.

ALL. Oh, honey .... / She was just a bitch .... / Forget her ....

FROSTY MOONS. It's not like I haven't been attacked before ... but it's always been for doing porn and being gay, stuff I could be proud of.

GERRY. Forget her, Frosty. She just wanted to talk.

FROSTY MOONS. But she told me I was going to hell.

GERRY. Frosty, look at me. Do you really think this bimbo, who spends her nights watching Heidi-The-Ho on public access, has inside information on who's going to hell.

FROSTY MOONS. *(After a moment.)* No.

GERRY. Well, then don't dramatize this. Use it. Take this experience, this thing you're feeling right now, and file it away, so that when you're doing a scene you can remember how hurt you feel, how victimized. Use it for your art not your life.

(The lights fade out as he speaks and focuses in on HEIDI-THE-HO ... who walks thoughtfully downstage.)

HEIDI-THE-HO. "Your lover Mr. Carlysle is here. And he's brought another man." *(The glider panel closes; she pretends to dust it.)* "Your lover Mr. Carlysle is here. And he's brought another man."

Bzzzzz. *(She frowns.)* Who is it? *(Steps behind the panel; we hear her voice.)* "Mr. Carlysle! You're here! And you've brought another man."

HEIDI-THE-HO. *(Steps out again, wearily tying on an apron.)* "I suppose that means I have to set another plate and pick up some more food for dinner."

GUY'S VOICE. That's not the line. That's not in here.

(The glider panel opens as he speaks revealing GERRY, FROSTY, JIMBO, and VIXEN rehearsing in the garage.)

GUY. Did you add that, Gerry? I don't have that in the new script.

GERRY. Calm down. It's an ad lib but it's not a bad line.

FROSTY MOONS. Well, if she says that I can't say "My God, Ted is still warm in his grave and already Carlysle is demanding a manage a twer ...."

GUY and GERRY. Trois!

GERRY. Yes, you can. People don't always answer each other. Melissa might be so wrapped up in her own troubles she doesn't hear Tina's grumbling.

HEIDI-THE-HO. I don't think it's grumbling. I talked to a lot of maids who work full time and they all say they have to do everything—the cleaning, the shopping, the laundry, a lot of times the cooking ... so when another person shows up and the table is only set for two people and all of a sudden Tina's got to reset the table and buy more food ....

FROSTY MOONS. But I'm only one person. You're only cleaning and cooking and doing all that for one person.

HEIDI-THE-HO. No, I'm not. Not with Mr. Carlysle always hanging around. And before that Ted. And Benny until he went to boarding school.

FROSTY MOONS. Oh, like me and Mr. Carlysle never go out to dinner.

HEIDI-THE-HO. Oh, right. Like a guy like Carlysle is going to keep taking you out to dinner once you're his squeeze. And what about his clothes? Like he does you and he wears the same clothes to go home?

FROSTY MOONS. So what? So you wash a few extra clothes. For what I pay you you should offer to iron them, too.

HEIDI-THE-HO. What do you pay me?

FROSTY MOONS. I pay you .... How much do I pay her?

HEIDI-THE-HO. *(To GUY.)* And is she my only income? Am I married?

GUY. How the fuck should I know?

HEIDI-THE-HO. All the maids I talked to had kids.

GERRY. These are all good questions....

GUY. No, they're not.

GERRY. I think they are, Guy. They're an exploration of character and text.

GUY. Gerry, can I talk to you for a minute? *(To the others.)* Take five. *(Leads GERRY downstage.)* This is a porn movie, right?

GERRY. Right.

GUY. No matter how good or fancy it gets, it's still a porn movie, right?

GERRY. Absolutely. There's no metaphor otherwise.

GUY. And we want to shoot it while the guys can still get stiff and the girls asses are high enough to see the hole when they bend over.

GERRY. May I know your point?

GUY. So we're not gonna do that if everyone keeps asking bull-shit questions and arguing about their lines. Put 'em back on full doses of whatever they're taking and let's GO.

GERRY. Guy, I was brought in because the cast wanted a movie that had meaning and intelligence....

GUY. Well, fuck what the cast wants. They're fucking porn actors. Just tell 'em what to do. What's happening here?

GERRY. They're not just porn actors, they're porn stars. And if there's one thing I've learned from Hollywood Access, it's that stars are like lions. They obey you. Or they eat you. But they decide which.

(HEIDI-THE-HO appears behind them.)

HEIDI-THE-HO. We decided that if Tina got fifteen dollars an hour and worked eight hours a day six days a week—that would be one hundred and twenty dollars a day and that means that Melissa would be getting something like seven hundred dollars a week from Carlysle just to pay for the maid and why would she need a full-time maid for just her and sometimes Carlysle?

GERRY. *(Taking both her hands.)* Heidi, Tina isn't the usual maid. In Guy's flashback you improvised we see that she's been there since Melissa was a girl, since she was a girl. Why? Why, Heidi?

HEIDI-THE-HO. *(After a moment.)* I don't know. Why?

GERRY. I'm not going to tell you why. But if you read Flaubert's *A Simple Heart*, I think you'll know. It's very short and easy to follow. Meanwhile, I'll do a few rewrites.

(The gliders close and VIXEN, in a tiny leopard skin, is projected on the center panel.)

VIXEN.
Bang, bang,
Orangu-tang
Orange Wang orangu-tang
I want an orangu-tang,
Bang.
Bang, bang,
Orangu-tang
Orange Wang orangu-tang
I want the Orange Wang
Orangu-tang
Bang.

Gimme an o
bang-bang
Give me an r
rang-tang
Give me an n-g-u-t-a;
Give me an n,
Give me a ten,
I want those Orangu-tang
Men,
I wanna forneo
With big guys from Borneo
I want an orangu-tang
Bang.

(The panel opens on the Ho Show. *They applaud.)*

> FROSTY MOONS. That number should be in our new movie.
> GUY. With the orangutan.

(They laugh. HEIDI-THE-HO does not smile.)

> VIXEN. So Heidi-ho!
> JIMBO. Heidi-ho-ho-!
> FROSTY MOONS. —di-ho-ho-ho-ho.
> VIXEN. Yoo-hoo, ho. Looking for Heidi!
> GUY. She's picturing all those party scenes with Jumbo-Jimbo.
> HEIDI-THE-HO. *(Suddenly.)* I bought this book that Gerry told me to read—*A Simple Heart* and … it's about this girl who's born on a farm and her father beats her and everyone dumps on her—
> GUY. Sounds hot.
> HEIDI-THE-HO. No. It's the book Gerry told me to read. It was written by this guy … *(To GERRY.)* Flaubert's a guy, isn't he, Ger… Mr. Cameraman?
> GERRY'S VOICE OFF. Yes. Don't talk to me.

HEIDI-THE-HO. ... and she runs away and finds a job with this widow who treats her pretty good and she thinks that's great because no one else ever treated her good and she has her own tiny room and she shops and cleans and cooks and takes care of the widow's two little kids and she loves them like they were her own but then they get older and go away to school and they don't write her or anything because they're not really her kids ... and then one of them dies ... and she and the widow are heartbroken and the widow hugs her—just this once in their whole lives—and the maid feels like part of the family but she's not really. And, somehow—I forget how—someone gives the maid a parrot and she teaches it some words and talks to it and she and the widow and the parrot live together until the widow gets old and dies ... and now the maid only has the parrot and then the parrot gets sick and dies and now the maid has no one so she has the parrot stuffed and lives with it in the house on the little bit of money the widow left her and she gets more and more religious and goes to church until she's old and as she's dying she looks up and sees this stuffed parrot and thinks it's the holy ghost and prays to it for her soul.

(There is a long pause.)

    JIMBO. What happens to her?
    HEIDI-THE-HO. She dies.
    VIXEN. And she never had a guy?
    HEIDI-THE-HO. No. I told you. She goes to church and cleans and she keeps looking for people to love like they were her own but they never are. But what gets you is that she doesn't know. Her life is so bad before she gets hired as a maid that she thinks she's lucky.

(A tiny pause.)

    GUY. Well, that's not important. Because that's not what our movie is about. Our movie is about—partly about—what happens when this horny, hot little maid—a virgin—finally gets a tree in her forest.

JIMBO. Oh, wow. Imagine having a life like that and not knowing.

FROSTY MOONS. *(Slowly.)* Yeah. Imagine not knowing.

(There is a short pause.)

HEIDI-THE-HO. Okay, ho-watchers no phone-ins tonight but if you're watching, cuddle up with your loved ones. And think about your life.

("Eating Box Lunch" comes on, then fades out and they call good-night to GERRY, and walk solemnly out. GUY stays behind.)

GUY. Gerry, can I talk to you a minute?

GERRY. Shoot.

GUY. Heidi's show is pretty popular, right?

GERRY. Right.

GUY. And you wanna use it to promote our movies, right?

GERRY. Right.

GUY. Well, *The Jew of Malta* and the story of some old cunt and her parrot is not gonna do it. Nobody turns on a TV show to find out how depressing life is.

GERRY. Yes, they do, Guy. All the time.

GUY. Yeah, yeah, but that's the fun kind of depressing. This is sad depressing. This is the depressing that happens when some dipshit on public access reads a book.

GERRY. Well, I can't tell them what to be depressed about.

GUY. But why do they have to read this shit. What's the point of all this.

GERRY. Art! Art is the point. Art is our gimmick. And we can't make it work unless they know something about it. I have to prepare them for my rewrites, for stylization, for tragedy. I have to give them an intellectual and emotional language. I have to teach them how to act. This is a great trick we're trying to pull off but we're not exactly dealing with mental giants. It's going to take effort. Incidentally— *(Hands him a paperback.)* I'd like you to read *Death of a Salesman.*

GUY. What?

GERRY. You have to be in on this. You can't be outside with your tongue in our cheek watching us struggle. We have to share a common bond. Please trust me. I learned this at Yale.

GUY. We already share a common bond. We're in porn.

GERRY. Do you want me to quit?

GUY. What do you mean?

GERRY. I mean if you don't believe in me, if we don't share the same goals, the same vision, this won't succeed. And it has to be successful, Guy. I have a lot of things to prove to a lot of people.

GUY. You know I can't let you quit. It would be a wipe out.

GERRY. Then ....

GUY. Alright. I'll read the fucking play. But this is like when you give a guy who has one short leg a heel lift. If he limped all his life, walking straight can really knock him off balance.

GERRY. I have no idea what the heel lift is analogous to.

GUY. These fucking BOOKS!

(The panel closes. JIMBO, clad only in leather shorts, appears on it.)

JIMBO *(Prerecorded.)*
I stand up,
When I go down,
Downtown with you,
    Down in the mouth
    Until I'm goin' South

I stand up,
When I go down,
Downtown with you,

Out of control
Till I'm South of the pole

I get directions on the fly,
Hi rise erections goin' by,
Lots of selections I could try,
But no go,
They're not low
Not down enough for me

I stand up,
When I go down,
Downtown with you.
Down is the trigger
For better and bigger,
I'm up in a minute
As soon as I'm in it,
'Cause I'm one foot high
Every second that I
Go down town with you.

*(The song is over; the panel opens ... as HEIDI, FROSTY, JIMBO,
VIXEN and GUY applaud.)*

HEIDI-THE-HO. Great dancing. And you're opening at Whips
and Chains in the East Village tomorrow night, right Jimbo?

JIMBO. I don't know.

HEIDI-THE-HO. Oh. When then?

JIMBO. I don't know. Ari's been reading *Our Town* to me every
night until three in the morning and I'm beat.

HEIDI-THE-HO. For you Ho-watchers who only watch the tube
Our Town is a play.

VIXEN. I just started it on Tuesday. How far did you get?

JIMBO. We finished it last night at 5 o'clock and we couldn't stop crying and Ari just turned over and said "What's the point of anything if she's going to die?"

VIXEN. Who?

JIMBO. Emily.

VIXEN. Emily? You're kidding. That's me. I mean I'm who I pictured as Emily while I was reading. I die? But I just got married ... just before I put the book down.

JIMBO. But time went by. And you got older. And you died in childbirth. It just shredded me because all through the play I pictured myself as George and I pictured our wedding ... and then when Ari got to act three and you died I felt so bad. I still feel bad. Because nobody can change it. I made Ari look up the writer on the net and he's dead too so it's forever. But it doesn't seem fair. Someone makes you up and gives you this whole life and then he decides you have to die.

FROSTY MOONS. It sounds like something God would do.

JIMBO. That's what Ari said. He couldn't even get up to shave this afternoon. And when Emily says she wants to go back to her life for one day when everything was happy ... and the dead warn her don't do it and if you do it, pick an ordinary day don't pick an important day and she picks her twelfth birthday ... and you see her mom suddenly young again, talking to her like she was twelve and Emily tries to tell her that she's grown up and she's dead but her mom can only hear her when she's twelve ... and Emily says "Oh, Mama, just look at me once as if you really saw me." And her mom can't. Because she doesn't know. Emily knows and her mom doesn't. It really scared me.

GUY. *(Trying to fix it.)* Well, whose mother looks at them.

VIXEN. Not mine.

FROSTY MOONS. My mother wouldn't even answer my phone calls.

HEIDI-THE-HO. You know who never looked at me? My father.

GUY. Who looks at anyone? The only time anyone really looks at you is when you die. Like this poor bastard in *Death of a Salesman* who works all his life and his kids hate him and he loses his territory and after he's dead then his wife says pay attention.

VIXEN. When its too late.

GUY. Yeah. It's like the show we did for Marty. I'm sitting there thinking what a sour son-of-a-bitch he was when he was alive....

HEIDI-THE-HO. He was great. Okay, we're here live with the great Marty Akens' brother and Vixen and Melissa Ryan alias Frosty Moons and the great Jimbo J. and we're waiting for your calls ... 212-782-U-f-me.... *(A pause.)* Tell us what you think about mothers and salesmen and the great Marty Akens ... or anything. Just give us a hi-Ho at 212-782-U-f-me. *(A pause.)* Well, this must be a party night because we don't have one call. So you all must be getting lucky to-night. But if you get low, call the Ho. *(There is still no ring.)* So ... Jimbo ... we were talking about ... mothers. What about your mom? Looked or not looked?

JIMBO. Looked.

HEIDI-THE-HO. That's so great.

JIMBO. But I always felt like she was looking at me because she was interested in my wad. She was always walking in on me. It made me feel funny.

HEIDI-THE-HO. Wow. So ... Frosty—looked or not looked?

FROSTY MOONS. I didn't have a mom so I don't know. But my *Three Is a Crowd* mom looked. She saw everything. Once when she noticed I was getting too full of myself she gave me a dog to teach me about others.

JIMBO. I had a dog. I found it when it was a puppy.

VIXEN. One of my mother's boyfriends gave me a dog and someone fed it poisoned chicken and it died. I never found out who did it.

JIMBO. That's awful. That would never have happened in my town. I mean, someone would've fed it poisoned chicken but we'd've known who did it. *(Suddenly, to VIXEN.)* Oh, God, I'm so glad you're still alive. It was such a bad trip, your being dead. It was such a sur-prise. But I'll take care of you. I won't let anything happen to you.

VIXEN. What are you talking about? I'm okay. It's a play.

Jimbo, it's a play.

JIMBO. Yeah. But some day you'll be dead. We'll all be dead. Because time passes ... it's passing right now. It's taking us along. I better lie down.

(The end music jumps on as JIMBO lies on the floor. GERRY climbs onstage.)

GERRY. Get some paper towels and some water. Cold water. Go!

(They scatter. VIXEN kneels beside JIMBO and strokes his hair.)

JIMBO. And what scares me is to know that even while I'm saying this now it's not now anymore. Now is over the minute it begins. It's never now. The minute you know it's now it's after. Now. See? I said it and it's not now anymore, not that now, now it's another now... and now it's another now ... and now it's another now....

VIXEN. *(Patting him.)* Okay. It's okay. *(Calling.)* Where's the ice?

(They run back on with cups of ice and paper towels.)

JIMBO. It will all be over. All the little overs you set the stopwatch for ... finishing potatoes or running a mile ... when they're over you're glad ... but all those little overs are taking you to one big over.... Give me more ice.

GERRY. *(Kneeling beside him.)* Jimbo, listen to me. Men die and time passes ... *(JIMBO whimpers.)* ... but art lives on because art, as Jaques Barzun said, is the reward of civilization. And that's what we're trying for. Fuck "now" and what happens "now" and what you know about "now," it's "after" that we care about. We want to catch something that will reward us for toilet training and furniture and tax

returns, something that will redeem civilization. That's what makes
you immortal, Jimbo. That's what stops time.

(They remain looking at him as if he has spoken from the mount.)

GERRY. Now let's begin the journey.

END OF ACT I

ACT II

(Prologue: A reprise of "Eating Box Lunch" is projected on the center panel. It is sung as a group number and the words FIREWORXXX PLAYERS flashes at the bottom of the frame.)

THE COMPANY. *(Prerecorded.)*
Walkin'—the walk with you, baby,
Talkin'—the talk with you, baby,
Walkin' and talkin'
And eatin' box lunch with you.
Walkin'!—
    FROSTY MOONS.
—ho-hum,
    ALL.
Talkin'!
    VIXEN.
—so dumb,
    ALL.
Eatin'!
    GUY.
—yum-yum,
    ALL.
Walkin' and talkin' and talkin' and walkin',
And talkin' and walkin' and walkin' and talkin'
And eatin'—box lunch with you.

(The image fade to black. In the darkness the sound of wind and sea and birds are heard ... and the glider panels open on the garage. Standing center are VIXEN and JIMBO, gazing out at an imaginary sea. Watching them are HEIDI-THE-HO, FROSTY MOONS and GERRY who serve as audience and background sounds.)

JIMBO. I have deceived you.

VIXEN. I do not understand.

JIMBO. I have deceived you. I have deceived you utterly.

VIXEN. How can that be? Is it that though your eyes are full of love some other woman has a claim on you?

JIMBO. O, no!

VIXEN. And if there is, what does it matter? Do not tell me.

JIMBO. But I have a wrong so great against you....

VIXEN. I will not listen.

JIMBO. I am not who I say I am. I have taken you with lies....

VIXEN. What do I care now that my body has begun to dream and you burn in my imagination. *(He turns from her.)* Why do you weep?

JIMBO. Because I have nothing for you; nothing but desolate waters and this battered ship.

VIXEN. I would that there was not even that. Only you. Why do you turn away? Why do you look at the sea?

JIMBO. Listen ... listen....

VIXEN. I only hear the crying of the grey birds that fly into the West.

JIMBO. But listen. If you listen closely you'll hear they are crying out to one another with human voices.

VIXEN. But what are they? What do they say? To what country do they fly?

JIMBO. To unimaginable happiness. They're crying out that there's a country at the end of the world where no child is born but to outlive the moon. And we have to follow them there, they are our pilots. *(Calls.)* Let us set our sails toward the west.

(GUY, standing upstage, whirls around to face front. He has a red bandanna, tied pirate style, around his head.)

GUY. To the west! No, no. The men would return home now; we have found more than enough treasure. Let's go home.

JIMBO. I cannot. I am going on to the end.

GUY. It is madness. What curse has driven you mad. *(To VIXEN.)* Speak to him. He is going to his death.

VIXEN. That is not true; for he has promised me unimaginable happiness.

GUY. He is going to his death I say. And he takes you with him. Speak—he will not deny it.

VIXEN. I am going on with him. I stay with him.

GUY. If you go it is the end.

VIXEN. I am a woman, I die at every breath.

GUY. Then there's no help in words. *(To the SAILORS.)* To the other ship, men. And I will follow and cut the rope with my sword when I have said farewell to this man. For I will never look upon his face again. Farewell! *(He embraces JIMBO.)* Then farewell.

(He goes out. She peers after him.)

VIXEN. The sword is in the rope - the rope's in two - it falls into the sea, it whirls into the foam. It is broken. The world drifts away, and I am left alone with my beloved, who cannot put me from his sight. We are alone forever, and I laugh, because you cannot put me from you. The mist has covered the heavens, and you and I shall be alone forever. Bend lower, that I may cover you with my hair, for we will gaze upon this world no longer.

JIMBO. *(Draws her hair about him.)* Beloved, we grow immortal.

(They kiss.)

GERRY. Wonderful.

GUY. I wasn't sure about my attitude. I didn't know whether to be mutinous or apologetic or ....

GERRY. What you did was perfect.

HEIDI-THE-HO. I thought it was very authentic. And I've been with a lot of sailors.

FROSTY MOONS. Very real.

JIMBO. *(Smoothing her hair.)* Don't cry.

VIXEN. It's just so.... I'm going off to die with him. And I want to do it because then we'll be alone. Together. Oh, God....

JIMBO. That's not how I read it. I read it we're going someplace where we'll outlive the moon. Where we'll never die.

GERRY. You don't have to agree with each other. Art always leaves a little room for ambiguity. Yes, Vixen....

VIXEN. So did you write this for our movie or did you just write it for us to practice with?

GERRY. Well, it's on a ship so it's not for our movie. No, I adapted it and cut it down ... and did some word changes and moved text and typed it up ... but Yeats, basically, wrote it. I'm concentrating on writing the movie. Good work, everyone.

GUY. You know, I got a few distribution ideas I'd like to try....

GERRY. Don't try anything yet. First let's decide whether to release it as an art movie that audiences discover has porn or a porno that critics discover is art.

GUY. Right. So ... then ... when ... how long do you think before we'll have a script. Just ... because I have to figure out about child support.... And ... I mean, we all got expenses.

VIXEN. My mother's on me for her check....

FROSTY MOONS. Well, I'm cool. I know a real script takes time.

GERRY. That's right, Frosty. A real movie script takes three, six, twelve months to write not including revisions. I'm trying to finish this in six weeks.

GUY. So that's ... what? Maybe two more weeks?

GERRY. Yes. But let's not think of it as waiting time. Let's think of it as time we use to keep learning and growing so that when the moment comes we're ready. Okay? *(They nod, mutely.)* Next week's reading assignments are on the table. Your scene work has your name on it. Your reading list is next to it. Please don't read Harold Bloom or Wichttenstein until I tell you to. And from now on I'd like you to read the actual book instead of using tapes. I think you're ready.

(They start gathering their lists and moving toward the door. JIMBO moves toward Vixen.)

JIMBO. I can give you some money. For your mother.

VIXEN. Oh ... no ... thanks but ....You're not working either.

JIMBO. I'm okay. I'd like to. I would feel like I'm taking care of you.

VIXEN. You gotta stop saying that. I can take care of myself. I'm not like the women in these plays.

JIMBO. I know what you're like. *(He hands her an envelope. After a moment she, hesitantly, takes it.)* Thank you.

(Lights out. The tinkly sound of a cell phone song is heard in the darkness. A light comes up on HEIDI-THE HO downstage left, wearing an old bathrobe and rollers in her hair, and FROSTY MOONS downstage right, wearing glasses and a tee shirt that says "acquit Socrates." Both hold paperbacks and cell phones.)

FROSTY MOONS. *(Into phone.)* Yes? It's Frosty. Speak the speech I pray you.

HEIDI-THE-HO. *(Into phone.)* Hey! Good one. On the top of page five in *The Poems of Dylan Thomas*—what do you think it means; "After the first death there is no other."

FROSTY MOONS. It's funny you should ask me that because I've given that a lot of thought. I think it means that it's so terrible the first time someone you love dies that nothing can be that terrible again.

HEIDI-THE-HO. What a crock. I've had a lot of people die and I feel terrible every time.

FROSTY MOONS. Yes, but I think maybe it's like a metaphor. It means that but it also means more than that and it's the more than that that's true.

HEIDI-THE-HO. Oh. So it's ambi ... ambi ... it's that thing Gerry said art always leaves room for amb ... ambi....

FROSTY MOONS. Oh. Uh ... ambi ... shit! We wrote it down ... ambi....

HEIDI-THE-HO. Ambi....

FROSTY MOONS. Vixen will know. He said it to her.

(Light out on FROSTY MOONS. Another cell phone song plays. A light comes up on Vixen downstage right center, wearing a man's shirt and a pencil in her hair.)

VIXEN. *(Into phone.)* Yeah?

HEIDI-THE-HO. Hi. What did Gerry say art always leaves room for? Ambi... something ... ambi....

VIXEN. Oh. Ambi ... ambiulancey ... shit—it's on the tip of my tongue ... ambi ... ambi....

HEIDI-THE-HO. ... Ambiugity ... ambi....

VIXEN. Ambiguity!

HEIDI-THE-HO. Ambiguity! Yeah. Thanks. Dylan Thomas is really tough, isn't he?

VIXEN. Yeah. But I tell you—I skipped to Susan Sontag because I thought it would be like girl-talk, and after two pages Dylan Thomas was like a comic book.

HEIDI-THE-HO. Oh, God. We're going to know so much.

VIXEN. Oh, I have something so great to tell you. My agent called me today. "Where you beén? You gotta be seen to be hot—bla-bla-bla—you can make seventeen-fifty a day if you go anal, I got offers—bla-bla-bla." So I say to him "But if I go anal I can only make that much money once, right?" So he says "Yeah." So I say "Then I think I'll use *Vixen Goes Anal* for my own company and save myself ten per cent."

HEIDI-THE-HO. Yow. Killer comeback.

VIXEN. So he says "Well, that's not fair, and you don't have a company, it's over a month, your company hasn't shot dick, you're not even working—bla-bla-bla."

HEIDI-THE-HO. So what did you ...?

VIXEN. So I said "Yes I am working. Me and Frosty Moons and Heidi-The-Ho are doing Dylan Thomas."

HEIDI-THE-HO. Nice.

VIXEN. So he says, "I thought you were only doing Jimbo J. and Guy Akens."

(HEIDI-THE-HO shrieks with laughter.)

HEIDI-THE-HO. He thought Dylan Thomas was a porn star?
VIXEN. Can you imagine?
HEIDI-THE-HO. What an ignoramus.

(Lights out on HEIDI-THE-HO and VIXEN. Another cell phone song plays. And lights come up on GUY downstage right and JIMBO downstage left, both holding books and phones. GUY is drinking coffee straight out of the glass pot.)

JIMBO. Guy?
GUY. Yeah.
JIMBO. I just wanted to know—do you need any money?

GUY. What?

JIMBO. Because I'm not smoking or snorting or anything so I have, you know, extra. So if you need some, you know, for your child support....

GUY. No. That's all right. It's only a week more. I can make it.

JIMBO. What if it's longer? We don't wanna rush him. *(Reads from his book.)* "That in this tarnished world this shining thing ...." We don't wanna rush that shining thing.

GUY. No. Well, if I need it I'll ask you for it. But you hold on to it for now. Okay?

JIMBO. Okay. Did you get to the one about the guy with the wax wings who flew too near the sun?

GUY. Yeah. At first I thought how the hell did he get off the ground. But then I thought—maybe it's a metaphor.

JIMBO. Yeah. It's really neat being a company, isn't it?

GUY. Yeah.

(The lights go out. In the dark there is the thin, sweet sound of Elizabethan music. The glider panels open on a sixteenth-century pasquinade in GUY's garage. VIXEN saunters along in semi-wench costume followed by GUY wearing a fedora and carrying a whip. JIMBO, leaning on a crutch with a patch over his eye, holds out a tin cup into which GUY drops an imaginary coin ... then boosts VIXEN onto a stack of tires, sits down beside her, and cracks his whip as though there were horses in front of it. Through it all, FROSTY MOONS and HEIDI-THE-HO in marabou stoles, comment on the action by singing "The Whore's Song" from The Beggars Opera.*)*

HEIDI-THE-HO.
"If the heart of man is depressed with cares,
The mist is dispelled when a woman appears;
Like the notes of a fiddle, she sweetly, sweetly

Raises his spirits and charms his ears;
I once was young but am no more ..."
    FROSTY MOONS.
"Hurrah, hurrah."
    HEIDI-THE-HO.
"From sniveling virgin to burgeoning whore,"
    FROSTY MOONS.
"Hurrah, hurrah,"
    HEIDI-THE HO and FROSTY MOONS.
"Let life begin when we are ready,
Let age not tell us when,"
    FROSTY MOONS.
"When hips are full and income steady,"
    HEIDI-THE-HO.
"Let it begin right then."
    HEIDI-THE-HO and FROSTY MOONS.
"Dance and sing,
Times on the wing,
Life never knows
The return of spring."
    FROSTY MOONS. *(Speaking.)*
Life is a jest,
And all things show it,
We thought so once,
But now we know it.

(Lights up on GERRY at the tape recorder, applauding.)

    GERRY. Excellent.
    FROSTY MOONS. I could hear myself go flat a couple of times....
    GERRY. That's okay. The whores who sing in *The Beggars Opera* might go flat.

HEIDI-THE-HO. I was on key. But I took singing lessons. I wonder ... if we put this on tape ... if it could be the new opener for *The
Fireworxxx Players Ho Show.*

GERRY. We won't have time for that. Because today ... we're
going to start rehearsing the movie.

(There are gasps.)

GERRY. Your scripts are on the table.... *(More gasps.)* Go on.
Pick them up. Grab a chair.... Your names are on the title page. If
there's something you have a question about make a note and we'll go
over it after the reading. Remember this is not a polished draft and it's
a first reading ... so read it for sense rather than performance. And
you already know the first scene set-up so open to page one ... *(A rustle of pages, a scrape of chairs.)* ... and go.

HEIDI-THE-HO. "Your lover, Mr. Carlysle is here and he's
brought another man."

FROSTY MOONS. "Tell them to come in, Tina. Let's get it over."

HEIDI-THE-HO. "Oh, Melissa, I can remember when you were
just a girl and you were so excited about going to the prom with Bud."

FROSTY MOONS. "Yes. I was wearing my first high heels and
pale pink nail polish to match my dress. And when I looked at my
dad's face, I saw that he was ready to cry, and I thought this is what
he'll look like when I get married."

GERRY. "And dissolve to flashback...."

JIMBO. "Gosh, Mr. Ryan, I'm double-parked and I'm going to
get a ticket if Melissa doesn't get down here soon."

VIXEN. "It's gonna be hours. She's putting on mascara."

GUY. "Now, Kitten. Better sit down, boy. You have a wait."

JIMBO. "But my car...."

FROSTY MOONS. "Hello, Bud."

GERRY. "They turn. Melissa is walking slowly toward them, at
once shy and confident, as if for the first time she knows she's pretty."

JIMBO. "Gosh."

VIXEN. "Oh ... my...."

GUY. "You look beautiful, Princess."

HEIDI-THE-HO. "You look like a real little lady."

JIMBO. "Here. I got you a corsage."

GUY. "Why don't you pin it on her, Bud."

GERRY. "Jimbo puts the corsage against Melissa's dress and accidentally grazes her breast. He jumps back."

JIMBO. "I'm sorry. That was an accident. Honest, Mr. Ryan."

GUY. "We believe you, Bud. We know you're a good boy."

GERRY. "And we cut back to the present."

FROSTY MOONS. "Oh, Tina, it goes so fast. Dad is gone. And Mama. And being young. It's all gone. Does anyone know how wonderful life is while it's happening?"

GERRY. "Melissa leans her head against Tina's bosom and weeps. They embrace and bla-bla-bla until Tina goes down on her. Carlysle enters with Bud." *(He looks up.)* I've re-written this, Jimbo. You're no longer Bud's son. You're the actual Bud. *(Reading.)* "Melissa gasps as she sees Bud, now much older."

JIMBO. "What is it?"

FROSTY MOONS. "You look so much like ... like someone I knew when I was young."

JIMBO. "Who?"

FROSTY MOONS. "It doesn't matter. 'That was in another country; And besides, the wench is dead'."

GERRY. Your line, Jimbo. Please don't stop. Just make a note and go on.

JIMBO. I can't.

GERRY. Okay. What's the problem?

JIMBO. How can I not know her?

GERRY. Know...?

JIMBO. Melissa.

GERRY. *(After a moment.)* It's been twenty years. She's changed a lot. She's ... bleached her hair....

JIMBO. I would know her. No matter what she looked like. Just like I would know Emily. Even if she died and walked into a room and no one else could see her I would know she was there and I would look at her.

GERRY. *(After a moment; coldly.)* What if you were blind?

JIMBO. I'd know her voice.

GERRY. After all these years? All the whiskey? All the cigarettes? All the tears?

JIMBO. I'd know it. I'd recognize you, Melissa.

GERRY. *(After a pause.)* You know what? I think I'm just going to make you Bud's son again, okay? Yes? Guy? While we're stopped. Problem?

GUY. Well ... I have a daughter. And she's around sixteen ... and I'd never tell some punk she was going out with to pin a corsage on her. I'd pin it on her or her mother would but he wouldn't get near there.

GERRY. Well, Mr. Ryan's known Bud since he was a baby....

GUY. So what? He's not a baby now. He's got a car. He's jerking off. And he's taking her out to a dance ... and they'll probably do some drinking ... and park ... and she's all fixed up ... and you think I'm going to say pin the corsage on her and give him the go-ahead to put his hands on her? What I'd say is I'll break your nose and both your hands if you touch my daughter. What the fuck am I doing saying it's okay.

GERRY. Maybe you have a little thing for your daughter, maybe you're afraid to touch her.

GUY. Maybe you'd like to die.

GERRY. I don't mean you and your daughter. I mean Melissa. Look, this movie has to be shocking. It has to have an edge. It can't just be a long version of *Three Is a Crowd*.

GUY. Well, isn't it enough of an edge that it's porn?

GERRY. No. Because porn isn't shocking. You always know

what to expect with porn—it's just a question of how long you wait to get it. I'm trying to put the industry on it's ear. I want to enter this movie in festivals. I want to try and get foreign distribution. I want to get great reviews and an XXXXX rating and then try and book it in art houses and start a whole controversy.

HEIDI-THE-HO. Then ....

(She breaks off and looks around at the others.)

GERRY. What? Then what ...?

HEIDI-THE-HO. Shouldn't it be better?

GERRY. What?

FROSTY MOONS. Just ... she just means ....

GERRY. You're fucking judging my writing. After coming off movies that are orgies with laid-in Neanderthal grunts ... and trying to do Guy's script which is so bad it's funny—no offense, Guy—

GUY. None taken. I was just trying to write fancy porn. You're talking about a real movie.

GERRY. Oh, and you've seen such wonderful real movies that this is a comedown. Well, for your information—compared to most of the movies I've seen this is brilliant.

FROSTY MOONS. Oh, yeah.. Absolutely. And compared to the crap we make ... but just not compared to *The Jew of Malta.*

HEIDI-THE-HO. Or *A Simple Heart.* I mean, you're the one who gave me *A Simple Heart.*

VIXEN. Or Yeats ....

GUY. *Death of a Salesman* ....

JIMBO. Or *Our Town. Our Town* is ... everything. It's that thing you talked about ... the thing that redeems civilization.

(He looks at them for a moment.)

GERRY. I ... can't write like that. I can't write a screenplay that sounds like Flaubert and Wilder and Yeats. Those men were ... great. They were the great writers of their generation ... of any generation.

HEIDI-THE-HO. Do you need more time?

VIXEN. Because we can always work for a few weeks....

FROSTY. Or a few months....

JIMBO. And I can help out with money.

GERRY. It's not a question of weeks or months. It's a question of ... we're talking about the classics.

JIMBO. Well, then let's do them.

GUY. Yeah. Let's steal a classic and rewrite it so that no one recognizes it but it's still a classic.

GERRY. No. I don't think so. You have to be really good to steal something great.

HEIDI-THE-HO. Well ... aren't you even really good?

GERRY. Do you think if I was really good I'd be doing a porn movie?

FROSTY MOONS. Well ... yeah. Because of the metaphor.

GERRY. There is no metaphor. Metaphor just means you've written something you hope will seem more important than it is. Dostoevsky didn't talk about metaphor. Kafka didn't talk about metaphor. Strindberg didn't talk about metaphor.

FROSTY MOONS. Well, what did they talk about?

GERRY. It doesn't matter what they talk about. It's how they talk about it ... how they lead you to the truth—detail by detail, step by step, until they break your heart, until their world is more real than your own ... because they're more real, because they're the real thing. And you're not.

(He begins putting on his coat.)

FROSTY MOONS. Where are you going?

GERRY. I don't know. Some place where nobody gives a shit

about art.

HEIDI-THE-HO. I'm sorry. I didn't mean to embarrass you.

GERRY. Oh! This is embarrassing. Not only do I not measure up to the other members—no pun intended—but people are actually telling me they didn't mean to embarrass me by noticing.

VIXEN. Hey ... what did we say? Did you think it was good? I mean, what are we taking you down from?

GERRY. "Did you think it was good? she asked incredulously." Yes! Yes, I thought it was good! Not in the beginning, in the beginning I was just slumming, just pretending I thought it could be really good.

FROSTY MOONS. No, you weren't. You never said you thought it could be really good. You always said you could make people think it was really good.

GUY. That's right, Gerry. You talked about being pretentious right from the start.

GERRY. But then, after awhile, I started the rewrites and I thought—hey, not bad. I mean, not great, not the kind of great I'll be when I finally get around to doing my "serious" work, when I really do my best—but plenty good enough for this. Well, the truth is, there is no such thing as "serious" work; there's only work. And everyone always does their best. I couldn't write any better if I sat between Balzac and Dostoyevsky and stole every other word. You know that feeling that you have that you're the only one who really gets it? You don't? Well, you didn't go to Yale. You didn't spend all that time reading all that great literature and thinking, "Ah, I see how he did that. Yes, I've got that down now." You didn't have the gratification of offering your knowledge to the totally uninformed, the waiting clay. You know, you give someone a little light and all of a sudden you think you're the sun. And then you actually see the sun, it's pointed out to you by your former clay ... and you realize how little resemblance there is. *(Picks up his briefcase.)* I have deceived you. I have deceived you utterly.

JIMBO. Well ... wait a minute. You can't just go. You're the author. You can't just leave without figuring out what happens. It's like leaving everyone for dead.

GERRY. Take care of yourself, Jimbo. I really enjoyed meeting you. Take care everyone. Read Faulkner.

(He goes out. There is a pause.)

FROSTY MOONS. It's the end of the movie, isn't it?
JIMBO. It's the end of the world.

(The panel closes. An image of a prerecorded HEIDI-THE-HO appears on it.)

HEIDI-THE-HO. *(Prerecorded.)* Hi, this is yours truly Heidi-the-Ho telling all you Ho watchers that the *Ho Show* which was changed to *The Fireworxxx Players Ho Show* was changed back last week to the *Ho Show*...because *The Fireworxxx Players Show* is a no-show. *(She giggles; to someone out of frame.)* I'm sorry but that was hilarious. So watch us tonight—live!—on pubic access, channel 35! We're gonna have fun again.

(Her image goes off. The glider panels open to reveal GUY in the garage alone, packing cartons.)

GUY. "... cut the rope when I have said farewell to this man. For I will never look upon his face again."

(FROSTY MOONS enters behind him; sees him packing the red bandanna, the marabou stoles.)

FROSTY MOONS. Guy ....
GUY. You scared the shit out of me.

FROSTY MOONS. I'm sorry. I have something I wanted to talk to you about....

GUY. Look at the junk in this garage. And I have to get whatever I want out by the 30th. I have to go through every one of these fucking cartons.

FROSTY MOONS. *(Looking around.)* You're giving up the studio?

GUY. Yeah. What am I gonna keep it for? I'm not gonna be shooting any movies here and they're raising the rent. Fucking Marty. He made 2500 movies here and he was too cheap to take out a lease.

FROSTY MOONS. 2500 movies. He was a talented guy.

GUY. No, he wasn't. He just could work. He was born looking for a job. He was forty years old when he was ten. My mother was like that, too. She scrubbed, she washed, she cooked, she lit candles, and if you went to kiss her, she looked at you like you were crazy, like you were keeping her from crossing the finish line. And Marty was nuts about her. Ma this, Ma that. This is for you, Ma. And the funny thing is he wasn't even Ma's favorite. My brother Mel was her favorite. When she died Marty cried so hard at her funeral I can't ... even describe it. "My poor mama," he kept saying. She wouldn't have cried like that for him. Nobody cried for him. Nobody was even at his funeral. The family was down on him because he did adult movies. They took the money, though.

FROSTY MOONS. I was there.

GUY. Yeah. You were.

FROSTY MOONS. And Jimbo and Heidi and the twins.

GUY. Yeah.

FROSTY MOONS. And you were there.

GUY. Yeah. I was. I was there for old Marty. *(He begins to sob; she puts her arm around him)* He kept me in high school. Marty ... worked his sour ass off. I never even thanked him. *(He wipes his eyes.)* My daughter will never remember me the way I remember Marty. Because I only see her for lunch every other weekend. Life is so fucking hard to follow, it's just nuts that you only get one shot.

FROSTY MOONS. Isn't it? And then you screw it up. All my life I just let things happen to me. I should have stayed legit but Marty wanted me and no one else did so I just let it go. I lost my place in line. *(Grabbing his hand.)* And that's why you have to keep the garage and do the Melissa movies, Guy. Because we'll never get another shot like this one.

GUY. Like what one? This whole thing has been a total disaster.

FROSTY MOONS. But it doesn't have to be. Remember what a good idea you thought it was? Well, it's even better now. Vixen's talking about going anal. For the first time. How about that as a come-on for our movie. Melissa Ryan getting off and Vixen going anal.

GUY. *(Thoughtfully.)* Yeah. That could be a real want-to-see.

FROSTY MOONS. A real have-to-see.

GUY. But I don't know how to start....

FROSTY MOONS. You start by getting Gerry back.

GUY. I don't know how you get a guy back if he leaves because of himself.

FROSTY MOONS. You'll find a way. Because you're the guy who keeps it together, the cement. Oh, you'd be such a hero. You'd really make Vixen eat it if you walked in with Gerry. Then she'd know what a producer-director does. *(He frowns uncertainly.)* Oh, just do it, Guy. Now. Everybody's so shaky. Sometimes people get too far down and they can't get back up again. "Things fall apart, the center cannot hold."

GUY. Dylan Thomas?

FROSTY MOONS. *(Thinks; then:)* It has to be.

(The panels close. FROSTY's image appears holding a whip and wearing a mask, boots and a leather corset.)

FROSTY MOONS, *(Prerecorded.)*
Not so fast....

Oh, oh, oh, oh, oh....
Not so fast,
Oh, oh, oh, oh, oh,
Not so fast,
Don't do what you're doing so fast.
Make it last,
Oh, oh....

(FROSTY's image suddenly disappears.)

    HEIDI-THE-HO'S VOICE. *(Off.)* That was great, Miz Frosty....
    FROSTY'S VOICE. *(Off.)* Wait a minute. It's not over.

(The panels open to reveal HEIDI-THE-HO. FROSTY MOONS and VIXEN on the Ho Show. The shot on the monitor is framed so that the top of their heads are cut off.)

    HEIDI-THE-HO. Thank you, Mr. new Cameraman ... newest cameraman. Thank you, Miz Frosty....

(As she speaks the right glider panel opens revealing GERRY in his tiny, tacky room ... watching her on his TV set.)

    GERRY. *(To the set.)* Frame up, you asshole.
    HEIDI-THE-HO. Thank you, Miz Vixen. Thank you, Mr. J...
(She teeters; they grab her.) ... where's Jimbo J?
    VIXEN. I don't know. He doesn't answer my phone calls so I guess he's ... having a long party.
    FROSTY MOONS. You're kidding.
    HEIDI-THE-HO. Maybe he's dead.
    VIXEN. What?   FROSTY MOONS. What?   GERRY. What?
    HEIDI-THE-HO. Whenever someone doesn't answer the phone I think they're dead. That's how my brother died. I called him and

called him and he didn't answer the phone because he was dying. He O.D.'d.

FROSTY MOONS. That's terrible. But at least he didn't die of natural causes. *(VIXEN suddenly rises and starts out.)* Wait a minute! Don't leave me.

HEIDI-THE-HO. Oh, Frosty, I've just been so down.

FROSTY MOONS. *(Winking at the camera.)* On who?

HEIDI-THE-HO. No one. I just started thinking about my kid in Winnetka ... and my brother ... and all the maids....

(There is a knock. GERRY clicks off the set. The Ho Show *goes black and the center panel closes. There is a louder knock.)*

GERRY. It's open! Come in. Rob me.

(GUY enters, panting.)

GUY'S VOICE. Jesus, getting up to this apartment is like taking a stress test.

GERRY. Ah! Guy! The mountain has come. Move the duffel bag. Have a seat.

GUY. I called you. You don't answer the phone.

GERRY. No. Too many people have that number. I use a cell phone.

GUY. I have the cell phone, too. You don't answer that either.

GERRY. I can't figure out how to turn the ringer on. I also can't figure out how to get messages. I'm not good electronically.

GUY. Where are you going with the duffel bag?

GERRY. Elsewhere. Anywhere.

GUY. You know, this is very stupid, what you're doing. It's like some broad saying if I can't look like Michelle Pfieffer I won't take a bath.

GERRY. Is this like the heel lift analogy?

GUY. I just mean ... Gerry, let's make what we have work. A little fake art, a lot of real sex ... plus Vixen is willing to go anal. Imagine what that would mean in Cannes—a digital porno with a real heavy message in which Vixen takes it up the ass for the first time.

GERRY. Nobody likes my script.

GUY. Come on. Don't be a baby. You didn't like your script either. We didn't understand that this doesn't have to be art. It just has to be artistic. This is ... this is ... a whole new genre ... intelligent-bullshit-hardcore-artistic-porno. We're finding our way here. And maybe the first movie won't be our best. Hey, wouldn't that be something! If we could grow. Come on, it's all any of us have.

GERRY. That is not true. I have my inability to grasp the stock market or electronics thereby eliminating 85 per cent of possible alternative careers in the United States. I have my brooding. I have my drinking, my grass, my amphetamines. I have my girl who dumped me and is now having an affair with someone actually in production. I have my father who is stunned that I turned out to be nothing like the son he had in mind, my mother who actually expressed her gratitude that I wasn't blind or gay—limited expectations? I think so. I have my Yale degree, my experience as a waiter and public access cameraman. I have the superior smiles of my college classmates all of whom I outshone as a student and none of whom I can afford to eat with. Plus I have the disillusionment of my professors, the contempt of my peers, and the opportunity to fail in another cheaper city. And you're asking me to give it all up to direct a pretentious porno?

GUY. *(After a moment.)* You know, you're such a smart kid. You can start a sentence and I bet you don't know how it's gonna end but you just jump into it and hop along and take a chance it'll come out sounding right—and I like to listen to you talk because it's such a gamble.

GERRY. Thank you.

GUY. But you ... shouldn't do that with us. You shouldn't be careless with us. It's not right to take everyone down just because you got wax wings.

GERRY. Oh, please—not back to analogy hell.

GUY. I'm just saying ... we were okay until you came along and now everyone's on their ass ....

GERRY. Not because of me. You called me in, remember? You were in trouble when I got there.

GUY. Yeah ... but not like this. Nobody was talking about great. They were just talking about more lines. It's all this shit about art that killed us. And my point is—fuck art. Let's just "do what we will have come for, "Melissa." I know they whined about your script not being a masterpiece but as Faulkner said "Between grief and nothing I'll take grief" and believe me—now that they tried nothing your script will seem fine. I don't mean your script is grief ... I just mean it's not ... nothing.

GERRY. *(After a moment.)* You read Faulkner?

GUY. Yeah. Well ... I knew I was coming to see you and I wanted to be prepped. And last Sunday I had a lunch date with my daughter and we talked about her five-million-dollar-a-month private school. And she told me about the new math. And I gave her the Faulkner quote. And usually her eyes roll up in that way that makes me want to kill her, but last Saturday she was impressed.

GERRY. I got my ticket, Guy. It's not refundable.

GUY. Jimbo will give you money. Come on, just let us talk to you, Gerry. Hear us out. Don't leave without giving us a shot. We're so shaky. "Things fall apart, the center cannot hold."

GERRY. You read Faulkner, you remember Yeats....

GUY. Yeats? Fucking Frosty. She told me it was Dylan Thomas.

(The right glider panels close. The entire stage is concealed now. A single panel opens downstage left to reveal what seems to be an exterior wall with a window cut in it. The window is sufficiently high to make it seem like an upper floor. JIMBO stands framed in it, balanced on a ledge.)

JIMBO. *(Softly.)* ... and now it's another now ... and now it's another now....

(There is a knock; VIXEN's voice calls "JIMBO"... and after a moment, we see her through the window.)

VIXEN. Jimbo? *(Sees him; screams.)* Jimbo! God! *(She moves carefully toward the window.)* You left your door unlocked, honey. Ari will be upset. Let's lock the door before Ari comes home.

JIMBO. Ari's gone.

VIXEN. He's gone? When is he coming back?

JIMBO. Never. He left. I made him unhappy. Because I had so much to do after the author went away. I had to concentrate on everything. I had to keep Emily alive. And then she died so I had to keep her just dead because after a while the dead lose interest in the living. So I had to make sure time didn't pass. But time passed anyway.

VIXEN. Have you been dropping a little acid, Jimbo?

JIMBO. Yeah. It helped me to understand what I should do. *(He sees her hand moving toward him.)* STOP!

VIXEN. Oh. Jimbo, don't. Don't do this. It's so tough. And it just gets tougher. You don't want to leave me all alone with later, do you, baby? You said you would take care of me.

JIMBO. Yes. Oh, that's right. I'm sorry. I take care of you. Give my your hand. You can come with me when the message comes.

VIXEN. What message?

JIMBO. Listen! Don't you hear the birds?

VIXEN. You mean ... the pigeons?

JIMBO. They're telling us to follow them to a place where Emily is still alive, where we'll outlive the moon. Hurry.

VIXEN. Honey ... you've got everything jumbled into one play.

JIMBO. They're all the same play. Give me your hand.

VIXEN. I can't, baby.

JIMBO. Then how can you come with me? Oh, don't you want to? It's such a great place. And you stay with me, remember?

VIXEN. Yes. "I stay with him...."

JIMBO. And then you cover me with your hair ... and you say "I stay with him."

VIXEN. Yes. That's what I say. *(She suddenly takes his hand.)* I say "fuck my agent, fuck my website, fuck going anal, screw my mother and my teeth. I stay with him." *(She is standing on the ledge now, trembling.)* "I am a woman, I die with every breath."

(There is the sudden sound of a door swinging violently open. GUY's voice calls:)

GUY'S VOICE. Jimbo? It's Guy. Guess what.... *(Sees JIMBO and VIXEN on the ledge.)* What the fuck is going on?

VIXEN. He dropped some acid. I was trying to talk him down and he took my hand....

GUY. Too long a story. There's no time. I just had a meeting with Gerry.

VIXEN. What!

GUY. Yeah. I met with Gerry. He was packed. And I talked him into maybe giving us....

(There is a scream. FROSTY's face appears in the window with HEIDI-THE-HO behind her.)

FROSTY MOONS. What's happening?

GUY. I just met with Gerry. He was packed.... I can't go through all this again.

JIMBO. Too many people are out here now.

FROSTY MOONS. Heidi! Call 911.

HEIDI-THE-HO. *(Calling.)* 911!

GUY. Move back! Help me get him off this fucking ledge.

(As they struggle to grab him, the right panel slides closed and covers them ... as the other panels open to reveal the inside of Jimbo's gothic-modern apartment. For a moment we only hear voices.)

JIMBO'S VOICE. "The birds will leave. We'll miss the birds."
VIXEN'S VOICE. "The birds are in here, baby."

(And then the right panel opens again ... and we see JIMBO's window from inside his apartment—the reverse of what we have been looking at. Everyone's back is to the audience as they lean out trying to reach him. Only HEIDI-THE-HO turns away and begins rummaging in her purse.)

HEIDI-THE-HO. I'm calling 911. I didn't realize how serious this was.

(GERRY enters through the open front door and stands staring at the scene in front of him.)

GUY.	VIXEN.
Come here! Goddamn you!	Come back in, honey....

(There is a shout as JIMBO lunges forward and they try to grab him.)

GERRY. Jimbo! Stop! *(They freeze. Then turn and see him.)* You don't want to do that, Jimbo.
 JIMBO. *(From the ledge.)* Yes, I do.
 VIXEN. He's on acid, Gerry.
 GERRY. You don't want to step off that ledge.
 JIMBO. *(From the ledge.)* Why?
 GERRY. Because ... it's not in the script.
 JIMBO. *(From the ledge.)* Yes, it is.
 GERRY. No. I have the script right here.... *(He fumbles in his*

pocket, pulls out a wrapper, his ticket; sees the mail by the door, snatches up a flyer. Pretending to read.) "Time stops. Nothing that is wax melts. No one falls. The birds explain that the land where no one dies is in his own living room."

JIMBO. *(Narrowly.)* Is this *The Wizard of Oz?*

GERRY. Hey! Is there wax in *The Wizard of Oz?* Does anyone talk about time? Or falling? This is my script. These are my words. This is what I wrote.

JIMBO. *(After a moment.)* It's the author.

GERRY. Yes. *(Still "reading.")* "The man on the ledge—with the help of the others—climbs carefully back into the room. Carefully he puts his feet on the floor. He bends his knees and sits."

(JIMBO climbs in through the window with the others clutching his arms. He bends his knees and sits.)

JIMBO. Gerry.

FROSTY MOONS.	GUY.	VIXEN.
Gerry....	Oh, God....	We're sorry....

HEIDI-THE HO. Give me a popper!

FROSTY MOONS. Oh, Gerry, it doesn't have to be great. We understand that now. It doesn't have to be all that fancy.

HEIDI-THE-HO. I didn't mean anything. I just....

JIMBO. ... Maybe I recognize Melissa and I'm pretending not to.

HEIDI-THE-HO. I've got my first line down, Gerry. "Mr. Carlysle is here and he's brought another man...."

ALL. Good line! / Good start! / Nothing wrong with that line!

GERRY. I just came over to say ... *(Looks at their anxious faces.)* ... that's not the first line. I had it all wrong. Never do a punch up on a script nobody likes. No offense, Guy.

GUY. Hey, by this time—

GERRY. We're going to do something completely different,

something bigger, deeper, better—I'm toying with the myth of creation.

THE OTHERS. Great! / Yes! / Hey!

GERRY. And the myth we're going to start with is the myth of Icarus.

FROSTY MOONS. Fantastic.

HEIDI-THE-HO. What is it?

FROSTY MOONS. *(Exuberantly.)* I don't know.

JIMBO. I know! It's near the end of the book.

GUY. It's the guy whose father made him the wax wings...!

GERRY. ... and he flew too high and the sun melted his wings and he fell.

FROSTY MOONS. *(Impressed.)* That is pretentious.

GUY. It's better than pretentious. It's arty.

GERRY. *(Beginning to pace.)* And by making it Greek we can keep it porno because sex was very big among the pagans.

GUY. Sounds like a want-to-see.

GERRY. We have to stay serious, a little tragic, a little obscure ... for the critics. And here's the *piece de resistance— (They draw closer.)* —we combine the myths of Icarus and the garden of Eden. Adam is naked—poke, poke—Eve gives him the apple. And the twist is—the apple is not carnal knowledge. The apple is ... self pity.

GUY. Great. And they're naked.

HEIDI-THE-HO. And is Icarus in the garden, too?

GERRY. No. Icarus is in flight. And when Adam bites the apple and becomes aware of self by way of self pity ... Icarus falls.

JIMBO. So it's not from the sun?

GERRY. No, it is but it isn't.

FROSTY MOONS. *(Excitedly.)* Oh, a metaphor!

GERRY. Yes, but we're also openly, blatantly, saying that great heights lead to the sun and madness—and self pity leads to a thud and Christianity.

JIMBO. ... so ... Adam and Eve ... Icarus ...

GERRY. ... are all together! Yes! We're telling the myth of creation a new way—by blending the Bible and the Greeks. Our excuse? It's all mythology. What is myth but a rationale for why what is is.

GUY. And it's public domain?

GERRY. It's the fucking Bible, Guy. *(Points to them.)* Okay. let's improv this. Daedalus and his wife are going at it. They see their son Icarus, naked, putting on a pair of wings—

GUY. *(Simulating sex.)* Icarus, take care. These wings are made of wax. Do not fly too close to the sun or they will melt.

JIMBO. No, I will go only so high that I am above the grey birds ... *(FROSTY MOONS makes the sound of a seagull.)* ... and then so high that I am above the white clouds. And then I will go no higher.

HEIDI-THE-HO. Oh, my son, stay! Talk to him, Kitten!

VIXEN. Oh, Icarus, my love, do not go. For I fear that you will be drawn to the sun, that shining thing, and forget you are mortal.

GERRY. Wonderful.

ALL. Great! / Good! / I love this!

FROSTY MOONS. Where does Melissa Ryan come in not that she has to come in. Does she? I don't care....

GERRY. But she does come in. Because that's where the money is. Her birth is predicted by Prometheus and the gods release him from his rock as a reward for tipping them off. And we see from his prophecy that the gods will die and once the gods are dead time will lead ineluctably to Melissa Ryan and the 50's. And the pentium chip. And Tina's announcement that Carlysle is here and he's brought another man.

HEIDI-THE-HO. Fabulous.

GUY. What were we worried about?

VIXEN. I think it's really interesting.

GUY. Cheap costumes. Togas and fig leafs and ... nothing.

FROSTY MOONS. This is better than ... easier than ... any of the other stuff.

HEIDI-THE-HO. Way easier.
VIXEN. And it will work just as well as ... anything.
ALL. Oh, yes! / Better! / Much better!

(There is a pause. Then:)

JIMBO. But it won't stop time, will it?
GERRY. No.
HEIDI-THE-HO. It won't be that shining thing.
GERRY. No.
JIMBO. And we won't redeem civilization.
GERRY. No.

(There is another pause.)

JIMBO. I wonder what it would have been like to be one of them
... one of the ones who are the reward of civilization.
GERRY. It would have been like pain, a lifetime of pain and re-
jection and rage and despair—and then every once in a while—
unimaginable happiness.

(A billowing, sheer, curtain drops, like a shade, and the images of
GUY, FROSTY MOONS, JIMBO, HEIDI-THE-HO and VIXEN
fade up on it. They are dressed in tiny, revealing Greek togas.
There is an occasional pluck of a lyre as they chant:)

HEIDI-THE-HO.
What was in the apple Adam ate
That laid him low,
The dreaded fruit that Adam ate
What did it show?
FROSTY MOONS.
What did he learn after that taste,

That made him sorrowful and chaste,
What did it say to him that he didn't know?
>   VIXEN.
It told him of justice,
And the concept of fate,
The awareness that "just in time"
Might come too late,
>   JIMBO.
It taught him self-pity,
It taught him self-hate,
>   GUY.
It taught him that what he was
Was largely what he ate.
>   HEIDI-THE HO and FROSTY MOONS.
Oh, Icarus, who saw the light
And fell,
From golden flight,
To after-apple hell,
We bid you now
Farewell.

(The image on screen fades out. GERRY steps into a single light.)

>   GERRY.
Life is a jest,
And all things show it,
We thought so once,
But now we know it.

THE LIGHTS GO OUT

)

PROPS

Act I

Ho Show
Two-tiered bench
Television monitor on cart
Wireless mic (Heidi)
5 black armbands (All)

Vixen's Apartment
Heineken beer can (Jimbo)
Table—UC
Orange chair and rug
"Bottoms Up" poster
2 bowls with pretzels—on UC table (Vixen)
Stack of black cocktail napkins—on UC table (Vixen)
Cigarette and lighter—on UC table (Vixen)
Black ashtray with wet towel—on UC table (Vixen)
Legal pad and pencil—on UC table

Garage
Cartons
Movie equipment
Car parts and tires
Large poster
Metal folding chairs
5 copies of Guy's script—blue (All)
Video camera and tripod (Guy)
Laptop computer (Guy)
Small garbage can (Guy)
2 cups with pencils and pads (All)
Cell phone
6 copies of Gerry's script—purple (All)

<u>Ho Show</u>
Bucket and maid's apron

<u>Garage</u>
5 copies of Gerry's script—purple (All)
4 Greek coffee cups (Jimbo, Vixen, Heidi and Frosty)

<u>Ho Show</u>
Death of a Salesman (Gerry)

<u>Ho Show</u>
Ice bucket with fake ice (Heidi and Gerry)
Water bottle (Heidi and Gerry)
Paper towels (Heidi and Gerry)

Act II

<u>Garage</u>
5 reading assignments—in Gerry's bag (All)
5 scene work—in Gerry's bag (All)
2 cups with pencils and notepads (All)
Bandana (Guy)
Wad of cash (Jimbo)
Keys and key chain (Guy)
"Crutch" sword (Guy)
2 small notepads and 2 pencils (Heidi and Frosty)

<u>Phone calls</u>
3 B. Behan paperbacks: *Poems and A Play in Irish* (Vixen, Frosty and Heidi)
3 phones (Vixen, Frosty and Heidi)
Cell phone (Jimbo)
Phone headset (Guy)
Coffee pot (Guy)
2 paperbacks of Greek Mythology (Jimbo and Guy)

<u>Garage</u>
Table
6 copies of Gerry's rewrites on table—red (All)
Crutch (Jimbo)
Backpack (Gerry)
Boombox (Gerry)
Fedora (Guy)
Short red whip (Guy)
Eye-patch (Jimbo)
Tin beggar's cup (Jimbo)
Marabou stoles (Heidi and Frosty)
Beggar's cash (Vixen)
Mug with pencils and notepads (All)
Laptop Computer (Gerry)
Scarf (Gerry)
CD's (Jimbo)
Yeats book (Gerry)
Tape recorder

<u>Garage</u>
10 or more boxes with junk
Box 1: Framed high school diploma, framed first review, bandana and
      miscellaneous junk (Guy)
Box 2: Guy's and Garry's scripts and miscellaneous junk (Guy)
Box 3: Video box covers and miscellaneous junk (Guy)
Large metal garbage can—padded
Box A: boa and Fireworxxx t-shirt

<u>Gerry's Apartment</u>
Bookcase
Desk
Large duffle bag
Scattered papers
Cot with sheet and pillow to sit on (Gerry and Guy)
Pill bottles (Gerry)

Stash box with grass and rolling papers—on desk (Gerry)
2 ashtrays and 2 lighters (Gerry)
Scattered clothes (Gerry)
Remote control (Gerry)
Paper cup and water bottle (Gerry)
Books in twine (Gerry)
Yale diploma—on desk (Gerry)
Framed photo of Gerry's parents—on desk (Gerry)
Framed photos of 2 girlfriends—on desk (Gerry)
Cell phone (Gerry)

Jimbo's Apartment
Piano with sheet music
Sofa
Jimbo "Jumbo" poster
CD Tower
Cell phone (Vixen)
Porn magazines (Gerry)
Mail stack (Gerry)
Cell phone (Heidi)

Video
Togas

Additional props
Gerry Coke Bottle
Shoe chair on spikes
Red cart
Shoe tree
Peg board
Red dairy crate
Blue stool
Blue crate
3 Vixen trees
Yeats tube with Skull

Poppers
Bagel on plate and 2 coffee cups
Zebra print blanket
Guitar case
2 Beer bottles
3 Jimbo Posters
2 Gerry Booze Bottles: 1 a quarter filled with water
Gerry pocket garbage: Plane jacket and ticket, snickers bar, tissues
    and Post-Its
2 stuffed animals
Green rug
2 native print pillows

OTHER TITLES AVAILABLE FROM SAMUEL FRENCH

THE RIVERS AND RAVINES
Heather McDonald

Drama / 9m, 5f / Unit Set
Originally produced to acclaim by Washington D.C.'s famed
Arena Stage. This is an engrossing political drama about the
contemporary farm crisis in America and its effect on rural
communities.

"A haunting and emotionally draining play. A community of
farmers and ranchers in a small Colorado town disintegrates
under the weight of failure and thwarted ambitions. Most of
the farmers, their spouses, children, clergyman, banker and
greasy spoon proprietress survive, but it is survival without
triumph. This is an *Our Town* for the 80's."
– *The Washington Post*

OTHER TITLES AVAILABLE FROM SAMUEL FRENCH

JITNEY
August Wilson

Drama / 8m, 1f / Interiors
Set in 1970 in the Hill District of Pittsburgh that is served by a makeshift taxi company, Jitney is a beautiful addition to the author's decade by decade cycle of plays about the black American experience in the twentieth century.

"Could be described as just a lot of men sitting around talking. But the talk has such varied range and musicality, and it is rendered with such stylish detail, that a complete urban symphony emerges.... Drivers return from jobs with stories that summon an entire ethos.... Thoroughly engrossing, *Jitney* holds us in charmed captivity."
– *New York Times*

"Explosive... Crackles with theatrical energy."
– *New York Daily News*

Award Winning!
New York Drama Critics Award for Best New Play
Outer Critics Circle Award for Outstanding Off Broadway Play